FINDING YOUR 100 PERCENT

FINDING YOUR 100 PERCENT

MIKE BIGGS

Finding Your 100 Percent
Copyright © 2021 Mike Biggs

All rights reserved. No part of this publication may be reproduced or transmitted in any form or by any means without the written permission of the publisher. All rights reserved.

ISBN: 978-1-956884-01-2

Contributing Editor: or all services completed by Imprint Productions, Inc.
Cover Design: or all services completed by Imprint Productions, Inc.

Printed in the United States of America
Published by Imprint Productions, Inc.
First Edition 2021

DEDICATION

This book is dedicated to my mother, Biease Annetta Grice-Biggs. Mother, it was you who believed in me when I offered no evidence of worthiness. You were able to see me in the Spirit and not just a moment in time. This allowed you to see my future maturation and not just my then foolishness. Your love for us and the community could not be diminished by your struggles with mental health. Your life has challenged me to fight for my 100 Percent and seek to be a, "Because of Person," to as many as I can. Without your love and support it would not be possible for me to have written this book. There are so many things you taught me that I wish I had applied years ago. But in my heart, I believe you knew the seeds you planted in my heart would blossom in the right season of my life.

To my son, Mike C. Biggs, Jr., you taught me more about finding my 100 percent during the last three days I spent with you before your departure. I will miss you and keep my promises to you.

CONTENTS

Introduction 9

Chapter 1: The Soil I Grew In 15

Chapter 2: Scotoma 19

Chapter 3: The Damage Caused By In Spite Of People 30

Chapter 4: Labels 56

Chapter 5: What Is The Secret To Finding Your 100%? 67

Conclusion 96

INTRODUCTION

Matthew 13:1-13

There is power in discovering what it takes to step into your 100 percent. Reaching your 100% is a combination of nature and nurture. It is the result of what may appear as many unrelated individual incidents and encounters, but is something more purposeful that will produce an explosion of unlimited possibilities to propel your quest. What I am about to say is going to either set a fire in you or will cool your jets. This book requires you to examine what your gifts and abilities are, then will address the need for you, and you alone, to put the work in to perfect it. Moreover, it will demand you become a conscious part of empowering others to do the same.

There is no graduation ceremony, no dollar amount in your bank account, no magical number of likes on your social media account that will validate your arrival at your 100%. No, it is just you looking at yourself in the mirror knowing that you have given your all to be your best self!

Invictus
By William Ernest Henly

Out of the night that covers me,
  Black as the pit from pole to pole,
I thank whatever gods may be
  For my unconquerable soul.

In the fell clutch of circumstance
  I have not winced nor cried aloud.
Under the bludgeonings of chance
  My head is bloody, but unbowed.

Beyond this place of wrath and tears
  Looms but the Horror of the shade,
And yet the menace of the years
  Finds and shall find me unafraid.

It matters not how strait the gate,
  How charged with punishments the scroll,
I am the master of my fate,
  I am the captain of my soul.

The Parable of the Sower

13 That same day Jesus went out of the house and sat by the lake. 2 Such large crowds gathered around him that he got into a boat and sat in it, while all the people stood

Introduction

on the shore. 3 Then he told them about many things in parables, saying: "A farmer went out to sow his seed. 4 As he was scattering the seed, some fell along the path, and the birds ate it up. 5 Some fell on rocky places, where it did not have much soil. It sprang up quickly because the soil was shallow. 6 But when the sun came up, the plants were scorched, and they withered because they had no roots. 7 Other seeds fell among thorns, which grew up and choked the plants. 8 Still other seed fell on good soil, where it produced a crop—a hundred, sixty or thirty times what was sown. 9 Whoever has ears, let them hear."

10 The disciples came to him and asked, "Why do you speak to the people in parables?"

11 He replied, "Because the knowledge of the secrets of the kingdom of heaven has been given to you, but not to them. 12 Whoever has will be given more, and they will have an abundance. Whoever does not have, even what they have will be taken from them. 13 This is why I speak to them in parables:

"Though seeing, they do not see;

   though hearing, they do not hear or understand.

NIV

     This is one of my favorites of the twenty-three parables of Jesus. In this age of prosperity, when this

Introduction

parable is preached, the focus is always on the seed. They concentrate on the yield of the seed and not the soil the seed was planted in. At sixty-two years old, I see a point in this parable that I did not see when I was younger. In my youth, it was about the crown and not the cross. I am speaking to my Christian friends, who are probably shaking their heads, and getting a lot of amens from non-believers. I am in no way starting this book with an attack on anyone attempting to improve their financial status. However, my aim is to shed light on the things which cannot be monetized that are equally as important. In seminary, I learned various methods of trying to understand the meaning of scriptures. I learned to process what I read, as if I were hearing it in the perspective of the original audience. The process is called Exegesis. Exegesis should not be confused with Hermeneutics. Here is a simple distinction between them: Hermeneutics is the field of study concerned with how we interpret the Bible. Exegesis is the actual interpretation of the Bible by drawing the meaning out of the Biblical Text. *https://hermeneutics.stackexchange.com/questions/36/what-is-the-difference-between-exegesis-and-hermeneutics*

    Now that I have cleared that up, let us return to Matthew 13. Jesus has drawn a large crowd. He gets on a boat to ensure he can be both heard and seen by the people who were there. He speaks to this crowd by using a parable, which is a story they could relate to by way of their own experiences. He uses the concept of farming. I know that we have been reintroduced to the benefits of having a home garden. Yes, it is desirable, but is no

Introduction

longer a necessity in America for getting our fruits and vegetables. However, that was not the case for those who Jesus was speaking to during this period. In those days, gardening was a necessity. For the original hearers, their first focus, like today, would have been how to yield the most from their seed planting. They would have missed the point of the types of soils that are found in the story and the importance behind that choice. Seed was a precious commodity not to be wasted. The yield of the crop could be the difference between feast or famine. Jesus wants us to focus on the process and not the outcome. The soil is the key to the yield.

    Jesus understood the results of the fall of humanity in the Genesis story of Adam and Eve. Jesus understood that race, gender, family of origin, and sexual orientation would have impacts on a person reaching their full potential. His focus is not quantifiable in economic terms, but the self-actualization of the struggle and how we respond.

    Even in good soil, the yield increases from 30% to 100%. Jesus pointed out that the lack of yield could be attributed to rocky, shallow, and/or thorny soil, as well as birds preventing healthy growth. Therefore, when he refers to taking away the yield, it can only apply to those who had their seed fall on good soil. My focus in this book is to look at the process of finding your 100%. Jesus is looking at making sure people understand the need to develop their gifts and abilities. It is a call to work and have awareness. Even when seeds fall on good soil, the garden must still be attended and worked. It must be watered and weeded. It

Introduction

must be fertilized to get the largest yield. I know city folk do not know what natural fertilizer is and how it smells, but those who have been raised in the country know what I am talking about.

This book will focus on the real work we must do as believers in our relationship with the all-powerful and knowing God. There is a universe of "yielding" possibilities. I am of the belief that life is not always fair, but that must not stop us from reaching our 100%. My life growing up in the south and my time in the military has taught me not to stop at the ugliness of a fallen world or give up because I must fight harder than some others to get to my 100%. I hope this book will touch you and awaken the will to fight in your most inner heart.

CHAPTER 1
THE SOIL I GREW IN

This book was conceived in the fiery furnace of the end of the civil rights movement and was born during the "Great Pandemic of 2020." The Civil Rights Movement demanded full recognition of the Declaration of Independence's assertion that all, not just white men, '...are created equal...' and therefore have 100% value. However, this book came to be during the pandemic. The pandemic has challenged us to examine how we validated and quantified the absolute value of one's 100%.

Matthew 20:16 says, "So the last shall be first and the first shall be last." For decades, many groups, from the religious to the secular, have declared the interconnectedness of all humanity. However, it has been embraced as an inconvenient truth by most of society. It has been so easy, until the 2020 pandemic, to be blinded by how we view everyone's 100%.

Never in the history of the world has this concept received the attention it has deserved. The medical staff, nursing home CNA's, sanitation workers, the first responders, custodians, fast food workers, teachers, grocery store workers, food bank workers, gas station attendants, and suppliers are being recognized as Heroes and Sheroes. Yes, the occupations so many have looked down on and are now seen as essential.

Coronavirus/Covid19 has brought the entire world to its knees. Orders have been issued in all fifty states mandating that we shelter in place, observe social distancing, and all non-essential business have been closed. We have over twenty million unemployed. The rich, the educated, the powerful, the saved, and unsaved have been ordered to isolate and separate to prevent the deadly spread of Covid 19. Those who society has placed excellent value and veneration upon have been placed in the unfamiliar unemployment lines; in other words: people that considered themselves to be "progressive" are now standing in unemployment lines.. As I author this book, over 30,000 people in America have lost their lives. A disproportionate number are the poor and people of color. This highlights the unfinished business of the civil rights era. It reveals the truth that society has not shown value to everyone's 100% by the lack of socio-economic opportunity, education, adequate housing, and access to medical care.

We all must stand in the reality of the need to pool our 100% to get through this alive. We are forced to acknowledge the parts of our society that we have given lip service to in truly valuing their contributions. 1 Corinthians 12:21 says it best, "The eye cannot say to the hand, 'I don't need you' and the head cannot say to the feet, 'I don't need you!'" We need everyone's 100%!

The question this book seeks to shed light on is: "how do you find your 100%?" Let me make it abundantly clear that I am not declaring that this book is "the end all be all" conclusion on empowering individuals to understand their value and purpose. However, I feel that it will be another chapter in the amplification of the intrinsic value everyone brings to this world. Before I lay out this process of "finding your 100%", I would like to put a few things on the table in the spirit of "full self-disclosure".

Abraham Maslow famously said, "He who is good with a hammer, sees everything as a nail." Well, you may have guessed by now that one of my nails is the Bible. I understand in these polarizing times, this might be where some may want to put this book down. For others, you may be expecting a dose of "Thus Saith the Lord". You both may be disappointed. When I first entered the ministry, I must admit that I had an "if I cannot preach the hell out of you, I might have to beat the hell out of you" approach to preaching. As I grew and had to face my own failures, I came to a more mature and compassionate view of the human condition. I once read an illustration that speaks to where I currently am in my faith walk. The illustration goes like this, "A missionary was sent to a country that stopped Christians from proselytizing. He was given a choice to stop or leave. He decided to stay. A couple of generations passed, and the country was opened again for evangelizing. The minister had died by the time the country had a change in leadership and allowed evangelizing again. A new minister was sent in and began to preach about Jesus. One of the villagers told the minister that he knew where this 'Jesus' was buried. He took him to the first minister's grave." The moral I found in this story is I should strive to let my work and my life be my sermon. This approach has been more of an effective evangelistic tool than an aggressive "take it or leave it" approach.

I have already stated that this book was conceived in the furnace at the end of the Civil Rights Era. You might wonder what I mean by saying "the end of the Civil Rights Era". The brand of Christianity I adhere to is one that Dr. Martin Luther King embraced during the height of the Civil Rights movement. It placed an emphasis on seeing the connection of the "Beloved Community "to justice.

The next nail you will see me use throughout this book is what I have learned from the great opportunities I've had to work with people with various, so-called "disabilities". Before I get accused of trying to be politically correct, I hope that by the end of this book I will have made the case that labels are tools used by those in power to simplify the process of not giving the validity to seeing everyone's 100%. This group is the most marginalized and ignored group of people in the world. To this very day, many are stripped of rights most "unlabeled" people take for granted. When other labels are applied, such as race, gender, sexual orientation, or socioeconomic status, they are even devalued more.

CHAPTER 2
SCOTOMA

The first point I would like to make in this journey to your 100% is: it is not a natural process. What do I mean by that? To answer this question, I would like to use both my training in theology and social sciences. (For you non-believers, bear with me. This will be brief.) Christian theology teaches that because of the Genesis story of original sin, humanity not only lost their relationship with God, but poisoned their relationship with the human family. We see the introduction of murder, which is the ultimate rejection of a person's value, recorded in Genesis 4:1-11. After Adam and Eve ate the forbidden fruit, they were punished with life ending in death. It was the end of eternal life as they had known it. They would start a family with two sons; the oldest was Cain and the youngest was Abel. In a fit of jealousy, Cain would kill his baby brother, Abel. When God comes to meet with Cain and Abel, he asks Cain, "Where is your brother?" The answer is brief, but reveals a broken bond. Cain replies with a question,

"Am I my brother's keeper?" In other words, life was all about him. He had no other responsibility but to himself. We all have found ourselves asking this question when we feel that giving something to someone else is asking too much.

This "all about me" life view was not the brainchild of Charles Robert Darwin; however, it is the cement that binds a secular justification of why we cannot value everyone's 100%. Darwinism is a theory of biological evolution developed by Darwin and others, stating that "... All species of organisms arise and develop through the natural selection of inherited variations that increase the individual's ability to compete, survive, and reproduce". In other words, there must be winners and losers for life to progress. It Is worth noting that this world view has been and still is being used to justify all types of injustice in the world. The worst atrocities the world has ever witnessed are the ones that are produced by those who combine science and religion to justify the exclusion or elimination of persons deemed not valuable to society.

This debate is in full view during the current Great Pandemic of 2020. The virus carried a death sentence to certain age groups and populations with chronic health conditions such as high blood pressure, asthma, and heart conditions. The process that the public health community recommended to slow the spread of Covid 19 required the shutdown of not only the American economy, but the world economy. The result is that over 20 million American workers are unemployed as I author this book. Many small businesses have closed without any possibility of reopening soon. The result is a sense of panic from some on the conservative side of politics.

Two of the most Darwinist responses have come from the Republican Lt. Governor of Texas and a Republican Indiana State Representative. As reported by USA Today, GOP Texas Lt. Governor Dan Patrick doubled down on his earlier controversial comments he made about reopening his state, saying, "There are more important things than living." Indiana GOP State Representative Trey Hollingsworth recently asserted that many Americans' deaths would be the "...lesser of two evils" compared to the economic cost of continued lockdowns.

Why is finding your 100% not a natural process? It is because of our collective "scotomas".

A scotoma is the Greek word for "blind spot". I was introduced to this word and concept while attending a certification training in '' Investment in Excellence'' at The Pacific Institute (TPI) in 1998. My cousin, Kent Hill, is a trainer for TPI and introduced me to the curriculum. Kent would become an unbelievably valuable board member at the charter school I would go on to start in the town I was raised, Talbotton, GA. Kent is a retired NFL player; I am immensely proud of him. However, if asked, Kent would say that I am most proud of how he has lived life in dogged pursuit of his 100%. Kent has shown a laser beam focus on reaching his goals.

I can say this is what attracted him to The Pacific Institute and its founders. TPI was founded by Lou Tice (1935—2012) and his wife, Diane (1935—2020). TPI was officially established as a corporation 1971, whose focus was dedicated to human fulfillment. Their work still lives on to this day. I am so blessed to have had a chance to see Lou and Diane in action. They were a team and a force for positive change in this world. When you can, I urge you to research "The Pacific Institute" and see their global footprint.

One of the main tenets of "Investment in Excellence" is a belief in positive thinking, taught by the discipline of cognitive psychology. TPI believes that our thinking either informs our excellence or inhibits it. It is not just about positive thinking, but is rather a process of challenging our internal beliefs, which are enforced by external messages saying who we are and who we can become. I see this distinction, because the Positive Thinking Movement, in both the secular and sacred world, has been abused. One of the most akin Biblical passages that shares the correlation between cognitive psychology and what is found in Proverbs 23:7, "As a man thinketh in his heart, so is he."

The Pacific Institute teaches that these internalized false messages are our "scotomas". They blind us to our worth and potential. If we are to understand and fully reach our 100%, we must challenge and cast out this "Stinking Thinking." It is not magical thinking that will produce unrealistic possibilities of our gifts and abilities. If applied correctly, the opposite will happen. We will fill our minds and time with working on the things that present our best selves. It sounds simple...because it is. Once we learn what our scotomas are and how they have held us back, we can move forward. This is a process and not an event. If we are not vigilant, they will return.

As I author this book, I am battling my arch enemy of a scotoma, dyslexia. I am profoundly affected by dyslexia in my spelling. I have no phonological awareness. My brain is not wired to see letters and correlate the sounds they make when put together. I do not write words, I draw words. I work extremely hard drawing the simplest words sometimes if I am not focused. I recognized I had a problem as a child, but I did not know how to identify it. The journey was a twenty-year process. Yes, I lived over twenty years with this scotoma, which controlled my life choices.

When I entered the third grade at Old Ruth Carter Elementary School in Talbot County, things were coming to a head in my young academic life. I am not sure of the date that I was pulled from the regular classroom and placed in Special Education. Somehow, I likened this moment to what it must have been like to be snatched from your village in Africa and placed on a slave ship. Now, I know this may sound overly dramatic, but it felt that way to a third grader who was already physically different. I had straight hair, green eyes and was about two inches taller than most in my class. It was not cool being light skinned during the rise of the Black Power Movement. By the time I made the varsity basketball team, my nickname was "White Boy". I will unpack that later in this book. Being placed in Special Ed was just another statement that I was different, but not in an effective way.

The sequence of that day is still fresh in my mind. The order to leave the group that I was working so hard to be a part of was delivered by our most beloved guidance counselor, Mr. Richard Chitty. The Chitty family were some of the most respected educators in Talbot County. Mr. Chitty's wife, Lois Chitty, was the Home Economics teacher. If you had a daughter, she would have to go through Mrs. Chitty to graduate. This included a formal dinner, using real silverware (which she would supply if you did not have a set), with your family. More devastating to me was the fact that their daughter, Eleanor, was in my class. She was the smartest and the leader of a quintessential "girl pack". I would snatch her spelling test off her desk and still flunk, while she would get an A+. I knew that being placed in Special Ed would confirm to her that I was as dumb as a sack of rocks.

    Mr. Chitty was known for carrying a pocket sized spiral notebook in his front shirt pocket. It was the same kind that the detectives on all of the police shows carried. All students knew that if your name was in the book, it was not going to end well. He came into Mrs. Harvey's third grade classroom and pulled out "The Notebook of Death". I knew someone was in trouble. I never dreamed I would be swept up in the raid. Mr. Chitty's list was in alphabetical order, therefore, I was the third name called. Once the list of names was read, we were marched to the "Room of Isolation", located in the elementary library. We learned in that room, took our lunches in that room, and we went to recess together. In other words, we were in total isolation. Today, we call these "Self-Contained Classrooms". It did not take me long to figure out that if I were to get out of there, I had to produce a plan.

As I stated, reaching your 100% is not a natural process. Our scotomas come from both external and internal messaging. The day I was placed in the Special Education class, I became blind to my gifts and abilities. I received the message and believed that something was wrong with me. Special Ed, as an educational discipline, was in its infancy. My "disability" had not been named yet. However, it was clear that I was not on the same grade level as my peers. I felt like even more of a failure because my older siblings, Ron and Angela, were considered academically "above average". So was most of my family. This story will not end with a miracle; I won't be able to win a spelling bee someday. However, it would lead to my understanding that not being able to do one thing should not blind me to discovering the many things I could do.

The rate at which we reach awareness of our 100% will be based on how we respond to the messages we receive from two types of people. I call them "Because Of" and "In Spite Of" people. The "Because Of" crowd helps us to identify the scotomas we or others have placed on us that hinders our search for our 100%. They amplify our gifts and abilities. They provide opportunities and situations for us to exercise them. They refused to let us find refuge in the land of "I cannot". They share the paths that they traveled to reach their 100%. Most importantly, they share with us how they removed their scotomas. You would think that you would find an endless supply of "Because of" people in your life journey to perfecting your 100%. I am ashamed to report that they can often be far and few between. They will not always appear in places or situations you expect. In other words, this type of person may not be found in your church, family, teachers, or coaches. You would think these examples would be the experts in motivation and direction. However, their own scotomas can get in the way of seeing your talents and abilities.

This leads to what I consider our greatest assets in finding our 100%; the "In Spite Of" people. The "Because Of" people teach us how to celebrate our 100%, but the "in spite of" people teach us to fight for our 100%. They are the ones who may not be wrong about what we will never be able to do, but they stop there. They give no thought or attempt to help us focus on what we can do or become. They revel in what we cannot do. Some will see it as their appointed responsibility to remind you of what will not and cannot become. Young people call them "Haters" or "Shade Throwers". Eminem, the rapper, said, "Behind every successful person lies a pack of haters." Drake had this to say to his haters, "I am what everybody in my past didn't want me to be." Social media is full of quotes about "In Spite Of" people. One of my favorite quotes is: "Sometimes, people try to expose what's wrong about you, because they cannot handle what is right about you." The only problem is most people react to and do not know how to appreciate the haters.

My intent is to expose the process of how we find our 100% in the face of a reality of a fallen humanity that says we should *embrace* the process of the "survival of the fittest". I am not advocating for a world that will suddenly become a "Because Of" society. This type of Utopia will not happen in this world. However, we must change what we have control of. The more we change what we have control of, the more the world will change. This is what we have power to control. This is where we get the biggest bang for our buck.

According to the Gestalt Theory, which is commonly known as the Law of Simplicity, every stimulus is perceived by humans in its most simple form. The focus is on grouping, and the entire theory emphasizes on the fact that "the whole is greater than the sum of its part." You may not be familiar with this theory, but it's like pictures of optical illusions you may have seen. These are pictures where the images appear to change over time as you look at them. You may only see a chalice and not people facing each other, or you may see a young woman and not an old woman in the sketch. We see what is the easiest for us to perceive first. Therefore, what every message we have internalized that focuses on what we cannot do will initially be how we see our abilities. That is how our scatomas work. If we only focus on what we *cannot* do, it feels easier for us to process than discovering the things we *can* do. Until we understand how we have limited our field of vision, we will miss the possibilities that lay beyond the blinders

We must understand that it is not about changing the world or others, but how we must change our perceptions of ourselves and the world. We must challenge the message "I cannot focus" versus "yes, I can focus". We must reject the implications of labels. We must resist the concept of "generational curses". These curses have been taught erroneously by some ministers and echoed in the secular world where life predictions are made based on zip codes. From birth, we are given messages that may not speak to our truth. What may be true for some, does not have to be your truth. There are certain outcomes that may have been true in family histories, but it does not mean that we cannot change the narrative. It is true that we are born into geographical locations that, due to institutional racism and economic neglect, will create challenges that must be faced. I am, again, not advocating for magical thinking. I am advocating for an affirmation of thinking in the possible. We must understand how history can blind us to the present and future, if not given the proper interpretation. Family histories will either fall into "Because Of" or "In Spite Of" influences in our life. We do not have control over how our life has been framed by our families of origin, but we have control over the picture that will be placed in that frame.

    Let us recap what we have discussed so far. We have stated that we are living our life with blinders on. We call these blinders "scotoma". We have had them placed on us intentionally and unintentionally. They most often appear in childhood but can appear at any of our stages of development. There are messages given by family members, educators, ministers, and others we hold in authority that tend to focus on the things we cannot do well. Once they are placed on us, we are not always conscious of their presence. The result is that we form a worldview with some elements of truth, but it blinds us to all truth. We have limited focus on the true gifts and abilities we possess. We arrange our goals and dreams around what we *believe* to be our truth.

As we encounter people along our journey, we are either challenged by "Because Of" people to remove our scotoma, or we meet "In Spite Of" people who will try to ensure we keep our scotoma.

One of the most painful encounters with an "In Spite Of" person was with my father. I went to Washington D.C. in the summer of 1973 to spend it with him. I could tell my mother was uncomfortable with me making this visit. However, she never spoke one negative word about my father. At this time, they had been separated for about ten years. My dad worked three jobs. I was helping him with his lawn care business and, evidently to him, I was more of a hindrance than a help. After not cutting the grass to his standards he yelled that I was "lazy" and would "never amount to anything". He died in 1976 before he could see the kind of man I turned out to be. It would be years before I was able to remove the scotoma this complex created in my mind and heart.

Thoughts:

*We must defy the so-called generational curse.

We must wake all the way up and take charge to frame our own narrative.

We have the capacity to change the "narrative" and those negative predictions) It may be truth for some, but it does not have to be our truth.

CHAPTER 3
THE DAMAGE CAUSED BY IN SPITE OF PEOPLE

Often, the reader of a book is left with questions concerning what prompted an author to write from a particular point of view. In fact, from high school to graduate school, many students are given book report assignments. This leads to academic expression of speculation on an author's intent. I feel compelled to help the reader understand my motivation for the genesis of my writing this book. Let me explain:

I first want to state that I am not trying to follow any writing style. I am a much better orator than I am a writer. Therefore, it is with intentionality that I am attempting to bring my oratory to these pages. I must speak from my experience to ensure authenticity on why I am writing on a subject. This chapter was not one I had planned on writing. I initially thought that it would give too much power to the "In Spite Of" people if I allowed them space. Also, I felt that would give the appearance that I was making excuses and blaming others for people falling short of their 100%.

What prompted me to change my mind, you ask?

Let us review what you have read so far. I started this book by writing "This book was conceived in the fiery furnace of the end of the civil rights movement and was born during the 'Great Pandemic of 2020'." I had no idea that this statement would force me to address that the conception and birth of this book amplifies its impact on the damage that is ongoing by people who are "In Spite Of", because of systemic racism. I already had the daunting task of ensuring that I keep believers and non-believers engaged. Now, I am going to throw in the second most divisive issue in the world! I must be crazy.

I have not been able to work much on this book because I became Covid 19 positive. I could have died before I got a chance to finish this book. By the grace of God, I did not have to be hospitalized nor did it affect my respiratory system. I became very weak, lost my sense of smell and taste, and I suffered the most severe headaches I have ever had in my life. I dropped 20lbs in two weeks. I had to go into quarantine for over three weeks. Each day, I wondered if my symptoms would worsen. The second event that happened was the murder of an African American man, named Geroge Floyd. Four Minneapolis, MN. police officers attempted to arrest him. One of the officers placed his knee on his neck for nine minutes, resulting in his death. It was captured by a 14-year-old kid using their cell phone.

His death has sparked a multi-racial worldwide protest, calling an end to racism and for police department reform. Never in my sixty-one years on earth have I witnessed such a unified call for change. This change is connected to a relaxation of racism and those who have been disproportionately affected by Covid 19. The rate of death for people of color from Covid 19 is 2.5 times higher than white people. People have been sheltered in their homes and have had time to hear from both White and Black medical authorities explaining the impact of race and what is happening to this community. Then, the world watched President Trump clear peaceful protestors from Lafayette Park and St. George Episcopal Church across from the White House, so that he could have a photo-op holding a Bible with his entourage. The peaceful protestors were pepper sprayed and attacked on camera. Next, came another video of white protestors being abused by police in multiple cities. The most recent and horrific video is the one that captures a seventy-five-year-old white man, Martin Gugino, of Buffalo, NY., being pushed to the ground by police officers. When one officer attempted to render aid, another officer pushed the officer forward. It was clear Mr. Gugino was bleeding from his head. These events have slapped the scotoma from the faces of those who had blinders on when it came to racism in America.

    It is becoming clear that one of the greatest and deadliest "In Spite Of" challenges you'll face in finding your 100% is racism. I am aware this statement may have some of you wanting to stop reading at this moment; I understand how hard of a subject this is. However, if I am to persuade you to examine if you are a "Because Of" person, versus an "In Spite Of" person, we must challenge ourselves to identify our racial scotomas. What

I want to avoid dealing with in this book is something I feel compelled to address: the ugly and divisive truth of racism. To not deal with it, I would be minimizing the contributions people of color have made in obtaining and utilizing their 100% in America.

    I would like to share my experiences in overcoming run-ins I have had with "In Spite Of" racists. The earliest family story I can remember is how my Great Grandfather, Clarence Caprils, was murdered by a white lynch mob on April 28, 1926. He was murdered because he had been accused of having sex with a white woman. I heard this story and connected to it, even at just five years old. That was my age when we moved from Columbus, GA., to Talbotton, GA., to live with our grandparents. We moved in with our mother's parents after she and my father separated. (Side note: They never divorced. My father returned to my mother after he developed Lou Gerig's disease my Senior year of High School.) It was clear that Talbotton was a much more segregated and openly racist town than Columbus. The N-word was used like one uses good morning or good night. We were told about all the businesses our great grandfather owned. He had a barber shop, dry cleaners, funeral home, cafe, and a tailoring business. He was the first Black man to own a car. He even bought his daughters a safe playing piano. Being the 1920s, his success placed a target on his back. This story made it clear to me as a child that finding my 100% would be hard and bittersweet. If I became too successful, it could mean a death sentence.

    Please let that sink in for a moment. In 1963, this

belief would be reinforced by the 16th Street Baptist Church bombing in Birmingham, AL., that killed four little Black girls. Medger Evers assassination in Jackson, MS., happened that same year. The very next year, three white youths who participated in the Freedom Riders were abducted and murdered in Mississippi for helping register Black voters. I lived in a state of alert. My mother and grandmother taught us how we should act in the presence of white people to ensure our safety. We had to be well dressed and always well behaved. We must not make ourselves targets. If you can, try to understand the weight of racist "In Spite Of" people I had to lift off my neck for me to seek my 100%. Think about the messages I received from the world that said my 100% did not matter. Yet, I pushed on, I had an Army of "Because Of" people who would not allow those messages to become my truth. Thank God for them.

    I want to mention two other incidents where I had to find the courage to "keep on keeping on". One came in the summer of 1974. It was a turning point for me and my community. It would mark the first in my life where I started to believe that I could find my 100% in spite of racism. In Talbot County, GA, where I had moved to when I was five years old, was still openly segregated in 1974. The schools integrated in 1970. That year, the schools were 70% Black and 30% white. By 1974, they were 90% Black and 10% white. They included me in the white count to reach the 10%. I say this jokingly because my nickname on the basketball team was "AWB White Boy Biggs". Damn these Green eyes! But all public places including the courthouse, restaurants, Doctors' offices, and public pools were still segregated.

This would change in June 1974, because Willie Carreker was shot in the back by two white police officers in his car. The officers said he resisted and tried to run away.

This incident was precipitated by the fact that Mr. Carreker was dating a white girl in Woodland, GA. This tragedy brought the outrage of an oppressed Black community to a head. The irony of Mr. Carreker's death is that his grandfather was lynched in 1909 for attempting to protect a blind Black preacher. He lived with his grandfather and preached, "Blacks must declare that they are free and must be respected." This resulted in the SCLC being called in to organize the protest. The effort would be led by a SCLS field organizer, Hosa Williams, who worked and marched with Dr. Martin Luthor King Sr. (Dad King) and Tyrone Brooks. These men would become the most powerful "Because Of" people in my life at this point.

However, Tyrone was the one that spent the most time in the county educating and organizing the adults and youth. It was Tyrone who taught me to hold my head high and not be afraid to look anyone in the eye when talking to them. In our family, good manners served two purposes. First, we were taught to respect our elders. It was what God expected of us. If we did not, and an elder told our parents, we could get a whipping. Secondly, when we showed good manners to white people, it could save our lives. It was clear that any white person could take matters into their own hands or call the police. Either response could cut our lives short. Conversations with both Dad King, Hosa, Tyron, and local leaders such as, Jack Pinkston, J.C. Walton, Sr, and Judge Albert Turner, empowered my generation to become free of fear. I am reserving the need to provide greater detail of this period in my life. So many played a role in this pivotal moment that I am saving the specifics for another book. Only a book can give justice to the Black fathers, mothers, and my classmate's willingness to put their very lives and livelihoods at risk to break the stranglehold of racism in Talbot, GA. Suffice it to say, due to their efforts, the overt segregation would end. However, there would not be a conviction in Mr. Carreker's murder. Overt segregation ended in Talbot County in 1974, but "In Spite Of" racism did not.

    I learned that the hard way in the summer of 1976. I graduated from Central High School; at the bottom of my class, I might add. My cousin, J. B. King Jr., ran and became the first elected Black school superintendent in Talbot County. His campaign would almost become my death sentence. By 1976, I had become very fatigued from carrying the weight of adulthood while still being a teenager. At the age of fourteen I was elected secretary of the Talbot County SCLC. In addition to my civil rights work, providing home health care for my father, and working in the dry cleaners after my mom had to quit to help care for my father, I was depleted. I had begun to turn to weed, sex. and alcohol to numb my pain. I was so exhausted, and I wanted a break. I wanted to be a normal teenager. I had made my mind up to join the Navy as my father did in World War II. I graduated from high school at seventeen because I entered the first grade at five years old. In order for me to join the military at seventeen, I needed parental approval. However, on April 21st, the day my mom was supposed to sign the papers for my entry service, my father died. My mom begged me not to go into service. Going to Clark College (Clark-Atlanta University now) was my back up plan. I could get accepted even with my low GPA and SAT scores because my sister graduated from Clark in 1974. I knew this was something I was not prepared for. I was so morally conflicted. But on August 7th, an "In Spite Of" racial bomb exploded in my life.

  I was leaving a painting job when three of my, what I considered to be, true white friends drove up as I walked home. I will not name them at this time. However, many in Talbot County that were my peers know who they are. They asked me to get in the car so we could get high. I said I would have to pass because I was dog-butt tired. The next thing I knew, one of the guys in the front seat pointed a shot gun at me and said, "Nigger get in the car. We have some business with you." With a combination of fear and disbelief, I got in the car. They gave me a pill and told me to swallow it. To this day, I have no idea what it was. All I know is that we ended up on a dirt road in an area I had never been. All during the ride, they explained that they felt "I was not showing respect to Mrs. Rowe, who was running against my cousin J. B. King for superintendent of schools, and for all she had done for Black folk while she has been in office". I had made my mind up that I would not get involved in the election because I did like both and knew it did not matter who I supported. I did not see the issue and I thought I could take a vacation from racial politics. I was wrong.

They would go on to explain to me why white people were superior to Black people. Then, they put a rope around my neck and made me stand on a peach cart and threatened to hang me. I told them that many people saw me get in the car with them and would know they were the ones who killed me. I explained it would be hell to pay. I said, "This is not 1974." This must have made them think about what they were about to do. They took me down and put me back in the car. While the car was still moving, they pushed me out in front of my grandmother and mother. My grandmother flashed back to when her father's body was thrown on their porch after he was killed.

Please understand that these guys would eat at our house. We drank wine together. We had talked about integrating the all-white churches they attended. They were the ones who had said things needed to change. Yet, when the reality that something their whiteness entitled them to was at risk, they were actually not "Because Of" people, but rather racist "In Spite Of" people. It was the most painful disappointment I had ever experienced, especially after the hope that had sprung from our 1974 Peoples Rights Movement in Talbot County. Sadly, it would not be the last time. I wanted to get our gun and find them. Grandmother and mother talked me out of it and decided to move me into my housing early at Clark. They wanted me out of the county. This pattern of finding out that your "white friends" really do not get it, is sadly the rule and not the exception.

The last incident I would like to present as a personal experience of dealing with racist "In Spite Of" people came in 2012, in a city in Georgia that I will not disclose. I was attempting to bid on a contract, and I had submitted a proposal for the Chamber of Commerce to review. I had a scheduled meeting with the Minority Business Director. During the meeting with the Director, I was told I had a "great proposal, however, If I had been white, I would have left there with a million-dollar contract". The problem was that I reminded the white business community of President Obama. I was too smart and could outthink them. I was a threat. He went on to describe an organization that his father and he were a part of. He disclosed how the older members would use "nigger" to describe Blacks in their county. He stated that he was trying to teach them better, but they were set in their ways. He apologized for not being able to help me with my bid and encouraged me to keep up the excellent job. I was in tears when I reached the car and told my cousin/brother what had happened. I could not believe this was still happening in this century. However, we could tell the future and knew that President Obama, with all he represented, was starting to create a white backlash. This was during the rise of the Tea Party Movement. The Tea Party Movement was a precursor to Trump's "Make America Great Again" movement.

Britannica describes the Tea Party Movement as a conservative populist social and political movement that emerged in 2009 in the United States, opposing excessive taxation and government intervention in the private sector, while supporting stronger immigration controls. The Tea Party Movement was a reaction to many of President Obama's policies. Controlling spending was a principal component of their tax platform. However, it was quickly abandoned when Trump became president to make way for his massive tax cuts for the wealthy, without any concern for a balanced budget.

In processing my life experiences that I have not dealt with in years, I had conversations with my ex-wife, Carolyn Peacock-Biggs. I know some will find it strange that we are still friends. However, we are. One of the conversations concerned her education and professional journey. I have had a front seat in watching her remove the scotomas that have stood in the way of her finding her 100%. I have watched her earn her associate degree at Pasadena City College, her bachelor's degree at USC, and receive her master's in social work at USC. She recently began the first step in becoming a Licensed Clinical Social Worker. The first step for her was to take and pass the California Law and Ethics mandatory test for Social Workers. Carolyn shared with me her struggle getting past all the racist "In Spite Of" events that caused her to not see herself as capable of accomplishing what she has. She recited to me how, in spite of receiving a quality education leading up to college, she credits her writing abilities to the assignments given to her in college.

She was surrounded by "Because Of" people in her life that said, "Go for your dreams." She overcame the message that she shouldn't achieve too much to avoid the repercussions for not trying to just fit in. It is so hard for non-Black-Americans to understand that we do not start in the same spot in life. As Carolyn shared with me, I realized we must take our scotoma's off to have the will to move forward.

However, as I have reflected on these events in my life and others, I understand why we need the youth who have taken to the streets to push us to the finish line. We must make it hard, even impossible, for racist "In Spite Of" people to continue to hinder our 100%. When I started to author this book, I wanted to use a process that would subtly get the reader to ask himself or herself if they were an "In Spite of" or a "Because Of" person. I did not want the method to get in the way of the message.

This thought process is the modus operandi of my generation. We began to believe that if we show up and do a respectable job, behave, or show the same values and beliefs our white counterparts espouse, they will become our "Because Of" people. Clearly, our logic is flawed. We did not take into consideration how our experiences and what we must overcome to get to our 100% is so different from their lives. They cannot see or feel the systemic racist "In Spite Of" barriers we deal with daily. Thank God for cell phone videos that are forcing White America to see the struggle. It has removed the scotoma that made it comfortable to just say "I'm not a racist" and leave it there. This moment in time is pushing their comfort zones and has our young people, including Black, white, Asian, Hispanic, and the entire world, saying, "But your institution and systems are!" So, as my parents expanded their comfort zones when my generation spoke up for more rights, now I must also.

I would be doing a disservice to the reader and to all those who came before me and the millions around the world who are putting their lives on the line by demanding an end to the racist "In Spite Of" systems" in this world. This demand does not relieve us of doing the work needed to find and nurture our 100%. It will not eliminate the challenges that are built into humanity's tendency to create "In Spite Of" situations as opposed to "Because Of" situations. However, it will make it easier for "Because Of" people to challenge and eliminate situations that are built into law enforcement, organizations, businesses, institutions, governments, education, and most painfully, religious institutions.

It is simple, we live in America. We profess to have the highest ideals concerning freedom and democracy. We know we have not lived up to these ideas. However, in each generation, named and unnamed individuals have come forward to propel us closer to living in a "... more perfect union...". It is at these courageous times we increase the "Because Of" and decrease the "In Spite Of". The result is a stronger America... a freer America... an America that creates opportunities for all its citizens.

I make no apologies for adding my voice to this moment in history. Let all of us take a serious look at the things we do not speak out against because it is not our reality. I am almost ashamed that at the beginning of writing this book, I was so hesitant to really address how systemic racist "In Spite Of" people have set up barriers for so many to reach their 100%. I recently started reading Princeton University Professor, Eddie S. Glaude Jr's "Begin Again: James Baldwin's America and It's Urgent Lessons for Our Own." Eddie writes of an incident where Jimmy spoke to a group of students at Howard University who had put their lives on the line for the civil Rights movement. Jimmy could sense the frustration of how slow White people were moving towards equality for Black folk. He spoke to this group of young, committed freedom fighters as an Elder Brother. He knew the struggle ahead of them would be even more challenging. He knew the conditions of Black Folk were based on what he called "The Lie". He was referring to the belief that Black Folk were less than 100% of the value of White Folk. The "lie" was that we could not nor should not reach 100% of the value of White Folk. Jimmy ended the night of intellectual banter and jive talk with a challenge to them and himself. He challenged them to never accept whatever labeled them less than. In return, he pledged as an African American writer he would never betray them. In other words, he would not fail to call out the racist "In Spite Of" people who would try to keep them from finding their 100%.

It is an intimidating read for a beginning author for two reasons. First, I am watching Eddie wrestling with the articulate use of language by Jimmy Baldwin. Secondly, I am a witness to Eddie addressing many of the same issues that I am writing about now. James Baldwin was a critical thinker and writer. He lived with the knowledge that he was not only rejected for his Blackness, but also for being gay and from a lower-socioeconomic class. Baldwin would declare, "I never became a Black Muslim, because I do not believe all White people are devils. I do not belong to a Christian organization because they have not met the truth of 'Love thy Neighbor as thyself', or the NAACP, because of its Black class distinction that repelled a shoeshine boy like me." In other words, Jimmy had many scotomas others would try to place on him. He rejected them all.

Baldwin's race to his 100% was littered with barriers he would have to navigate, while trying to remain hopeful for a better America. The murders of Medger Evers, Malcolm X, and Dr. King would leave him with a lasting doubt of White America's ability to abandon their myth that Black people are not worthy of 100% acknowledgement from humanity. Dr. Stephen Casmir's "Did I get James Baldwin Wrong" states in Haitian filmmaker Raoul Peck's documentary, "I am not your Negro", both Baldwin and King move closer to Malcolm's view that it will take violence to change America. I think that Dr. Casmir misinterprets Baldwin's and King's thoughts toward the end of their lives. They are acknowledging the depths of the challenge of getting rid of the racist "In Spite Of" people. It is a struggle to not see your efforts as futile.

Every time I feel ready to move on to writing on another subject, life interjects itself like a living stop sign. It screamed at me not to stop, but to continue. On July 17, 2020, we lost two men who I had the pleasure of knowing and learning from, both C.T. Vivian and U.S Rep. John Lewis. These two stalwarts of the Civil Rights Era outlived Baldwin, Evers, King, and Malcolm. They not only outlived them, but fought on to the end of their lives.

I met C.T. in 1997 in person at Greenbrier Mall, in Atlanta. I say, "in person", because I met him in spirit long ago. Cordy Tindell (C.T.) Vivian's biography is found on the National Visionary Leadership Project website'(http://www.visionaryproject.org/vivianct/) They write this of C.T. prior to his passing:

C.T. Vivian says his mother and grandmother had a vision for his life. Despite losing their family farm to the Depression, a home to arson and their husbands, these women were determined that their son would become an educated, self-confident leader, and continue the family's progress from slavery. Because of this foundation, Vivian spent his life using his position to stand up for the rights of others and became a vanguard in the struggle for racial equality.

The only child of Robert Cordie and Euzetta Tindell Vivian, young Cordy Tindell ("C.T.") moved to Macomb, Illinois with his mother and grandmother in 1930. The women chose Macomb, because it had non-segregated schools and a local college. After graduating from Macomb High School in 1942, where he had been an active student leader, Vivian began a stint at Western Illinois University. He decided to leave college and moved to Peoria to work at the Carver Community Center as assistant boy's director. There he met his wife, Octavia, who also worked at the center.

In 1947, Vivian participated in his first non-violent action to end segregation at lunch counters in Peoria. But because of his strong religious upbringing and beliefs, he says he was called to a life in the ministry. However, he saw no separation between civil rights, faith, and ministry because "racism is a moral issue." With the help of his church, he enrolled in American Baptist Theological Seminary in Nashville in 1955.

Also in 1955, he and other ministers founded the Nashville Christian Leadership Conference, an affiliate of the Southern Christian Leadership Conference (SCLC). The group organized and trained students to embark on a movement to end segregation in Nashville. The Nashville affiliate organized the city's first sit-ins in 1960 and led the first march of the Civil Rights Movement. In 1961, he joined Student Nonviolent Coordinating Committee (SNCC) members and other ministers to continue the Freedom Rides into Jackson, Miss. after a group from the Congress of Racial Equality disbanded. The SNCC group was arrested, and Vivian was savagely beaten at Parchman Prison. In 1963, Martin Luther King asked Vivian to work on the Executive Staff of the SCLC as the national director of affiliates. As an SCLC strategist, he worked to help get the Civil Rights Bill and Voting Rights Acts passed. In 1965, he famously confronted Sheriff Jim Clark on the steps of Selma's courthouse while leading Blacks to register to vote.

After leaving SCLC in 1966, he moved to Chicago to direct the Urban Training Center for Christian Missions where he trained clergy, community leaders and others to organize. Later, as a coordinator for the Coalition for United Community Action, he led a direct-action campaign against racism in trade unions and helped mediate a truce among Chicago gangs. In 1972, he became the director of Seminary Without Walls at Shaw University Divinity School in Raleigh, N.C.

Among his many leadership roles, he serves on the board of the Center for Democratic Renewal, the National Voting Rights Museum, and as a founder of Capital City Bank, a Black-owned bank in Atlanta. He has provided civil rights counsel to Presidents Johnson, Carter, Reagan, and Clinton and continues to lecture on racial justice and democracy. He resides in Atlanta.

My personal biography of times with C.T. is punctuated with his humility, wisdom, and inspiration. While having coffee at the food court in Greenbrier, I shared with him the conversion I had with Daddy King, when he conducted my great Aunt Willie's funeral in 1980. I told him I would like to ask him the same question that I asked Daddy King concerning his faith and hope in the face of so much pain and loss. King had said, "It takes too much energy to quit." C.T. asked me if I understood what Daddy King was saying, and I said that I believe I did. C.T. said, "Let me help you. He meant that if you give in to hate or despair, you will have to surrender to a state of helplessness. You will have to abandon your power to change the world you live in. You will have to give up the notion that your gifts and abilities have no value and accept that you do not matter to God." He then quoted 2 Timothy 4:7, "I have fought the good fight, I have finished the race, I have kept the faith." He said this embodied what the Civil Rights Era was about. God only asks you to do your part in making the world a better place. C.T. raised over $500,000.00 to save Morris Brown College in Atlanta. Morris Brown is now fully functioning and is experiencing its own renaissance, strictly because of his work. Now you know why Dr. King called him the greatest preacher of all time.

This conversation on keeping the faith must be bookended with the life of John Lewis. I first met John in 1974 and I was introduced to him by Tyron Brooks. However, I would get a chance to work with him more closely when returning to Clark College in 1986 after leaving the Army. John was in a heated race for the U. S. Representative position for Georgia's 5th Congressional District against Julian Bond, his former Student Nonviolent Coordinating Committee (SNCC) colleague. These two were men I had respected my whole life. But choices had to be made. Julian's family background was a vast contrast to John's. The Encyclopedia of World biography offers this view of his family of origins:

Horace Julian Bond, born on January 14, 1940, in Nashville, Tennessee, was the descendant of several generations of Black educators and preachers. When his father Horace Mann Bond became president of Lincoln University in Oxford, Pennsylvania, the family moved into an environment that was mostly White. While in Oxford, the elder Bond caused a stir because of his protests segregated facilities (people being required to use different facilities based on their race) and White attitudes of racial superiority. Young Julian, however, adjusted easily to his pristine environment. He attended elementary school with White children and won the sixth-grade award for being the brightest student in the class. He was sent to George School, near Philadelphia, Pennsylvania, for his high-school education. He encountered a few instances of racial prejudice (being judged because of his race) during these years, but overall, he adjusted well to the academic environment—although his grades were only average. His father later became president of Atlanta University and the family moved to Atlanta, Georgia. Despite rumors of racial unrest, Bond decided to attend Morehouse College in Atlanta after his graduation from high school He started college.

https://www.notablebiographies.com/Be-Br/Bond-Julian.html#ixzz6T8efiKPB

In contrast, John's birth was of a more humble origin. His biography that appears on his congressional website records:

He was born the son of sharecroppers on February 21, 1940, outside of Troy, Alabama. He grew up on his family's farm and attended segregated public schools in Pike County, Alabama. As a young boy, he was inspired by the activism surrounding the Montgomery Bus Boycott and the words of the Rev. Martin Luther King Jr., which he heard on radio broadcasts. In those pivotal moments, he decided to become a part of the Civil Rights Movement.

Ever since then, he has remained at the vanguard of progressive social movements and the human rights struggle in the United States.

As a student at Fisk University, John Lewis organized sit-in demonstrations at segregated lunch counters in Nashville, Tennessee. In 1961, he volunteered to participate in the Freedom Rides, which challenged segregation at interstate bus terminals across the South. Lewis risked his life on those Rides many times by simply sitting in seats reserved for White patrons. He was also beaten severely by angry mobs and arrested by police for challenging the injustice of Jim Crow segregation in the South.

https://johnlewis.house.gov/john-lewis/biography.

John would go on to defect his former friend and colleague. Julian had come under scrutiny for allegations from his wife that he was having an affair and using drugs. It was a very painful time for those of us who held Julian in such high regard. However, it taught us a great lesson on the subject matter of "he without sin may cast the first stone"!

John is best known for the beating he took during the March to Montgomery. The national Archives recorded this event:

In 1965, at the height of the modern civil rights movement, activists organized a march for voting rights, from Selma, Alabama, to Montgomery, the state capital.

On March 7, some 600 people assembled at a downtown church, knelt briefly in prayer, and began walking silently, two-by-two through the city streets.

With Hosea Williams of the Southern Christian Leadership Conference (SCLC) leading the demonstration, and John Lewis, Chairman of the Student Nonviolent Coordinating Committee (SNCC), at his side, the marchers were stopped as they were leaving Selma, at the end of the Edmund Pettus Bridge, by some 150 Alabama state troopers, sheriff's deputies, and police officers, who ordered the demonstrators to disperse.

One minute and five seconds after a two-minute warning was announced, the troops advanced, wielding clubs, bullwhips, and tear gas. John Lewis, who suffered a skull fracture, was one of fifty-eight people treated for injuries at the local hospital. The day is remembered in history as "Bloody Sunday." Less than one week later, Lewis recounted the attack on the marchers during a federal hearing at which the demonstrators sought protection for a full-scale march to Montgomery.

John Lewis would continue to work for change until the day he died. He has been discovered and embraced by the Black Lives Matter Movement. His courage and humility cannot be denied. He was committed to ensuring that everyone's 100% was valued. I am sure that Jimmy Baldwin would have been encouraged by his work with LGBTQ rights. He never gave up on Dr. King's principles of nonviolent intervention. He was never discouraged by setbacks; the gutting of the 1965 Voters Rights Act that he shed his blood for in 2013 being one of them. He credited his sharecropping background for his willingness to work hard. My experience with John was his natural ability to recognize and validate your 100%. In 1998, when I started the Talbot County Charter Alternative Academy, I needed his help in getting funding. John made it clear he was not a supporter of Charter Schools. However, he acknowledged that this was the only way I could get funding to serve the sixty plus students who had been expelled with no opportunity to continue their education. He made calls for me and did not try to block my funding. I will never forget his willingness to help a country boy from Talbot County to follow him.

Irony cannot be understated, as I am a graduate of Troy State University; the first college he tried to integrate. Troy would later award him with honorary degrees for his work. I do not deserve to be mentioned in the same breath as these giants of courage. I know I cannot sing a solo on how to fight in this battle against the racist "In Spite Of" people. However, I hope to be in harmony with the choir that has sung over the centuries the songs of "liberty and freedom for all". My contribution is that racist "In Spite Of" people will not and should not stop you from finding your 100%!

As I was nearing the end of writing this chapter, circumstances I am currently witnessing demand that I continue its message. So, I'm not closing it just yet. On September 20th, 2020, while I penned this chapter, President Trump was asked if he would condemn white wupremacy during the presidential debate with former

Vice-President Joe Biden. The moderator, Chris Wallace of Fox News, asked President Trump before a national audience to denounce the white supremacy group (The Proud Boys), who have perpetrated violence against "Black Lives Matter" activists. His response was nothing less than disgraceful and cowardly. He said "...stand down and stand by." Many, as I did, heard this as a dog whistle to the White Supremacy groups in America that Trump counts on for support.

Remember at the time that I am authoring this book, Covid 19 has claimed over 200,015 deaths. Over seven million are infected. This includes President Trump, his wife Ivanka, and over thirty-eight people who either work at the White House or have attended super spreader events at the White House. The President has been hospitalized and has returned to the White House. Upon his return, he has already violated the quarantine protocols created by his task force.

The results of his reckless behavior have placed Biden in a double-digit lead over Trump. Trump and the Republican Party are using voter intimidation tactics and pursuing lawsuits to ensure difficulty for Black and Brown people to vote. President Trump has pushed his agenda by falsely saying, "Due to an increase in voting by mail, we are facing a high probability of massive voter fraud." He has also stated that this is the "only way he could lose" and therefore refuses to quarantine. He has suggested that he will not support a peaceful transition of power if he were to lose to Biden.

This information updated in this chapter is not just

for historical context, but I feel that my reaction to these events is necessary. I have not been able to write because I have been challenged in my faith that a person, especially a person of color, can find their 100% in America. The unfolding events in this year, 2020, have rocked my faith like no other time in my life. This year feels like America is going backwards and losing her soul. Trump's grip on 45% of the county seems immovable. It appears that his actions will finally deliver the White Evangelical desire to reverse Roe vs Wade, among other antiquated agendas. This is what they use to justify looking the other way on his assaults on democracy.

In each generation from slavery to now, the White Church has failed to respond with the reality of the Gospel. Acts 10:35 states that God "accepts from every nation the one who fears him and does what is right". America has failed to see the scotoma of racism. It refuses to ensure the playing field is level. America has failed to see and address the discrimination that people of color face on their path to living their 100%.

I had to dig deep into my soul and reach for the strength of my ancestors, not only for my journey, but for those who will read this book. I had to remind myself of the many people, from slavery until now, who never gave into the ugliness of hatred and injustice. I found my strength in Ecclesiastes 9:11, "Again I saw that under the sun the race is not given to the swift, nor the battle to the strong, nor bread to the wise, nor riches to the intelligent, nor favor to those with knowledge, but time and chance happened to them all." We do not determine the hand we are dealt, but with skill and determination, we must play it to our best ability; the juice is worth the squeeze.

There is more surrounding this. Whoop, there it is!

CHAPTER 4
LABELS

Let us look at a biblical example of how labels are placed on an individual. There is a story in the bible about a friendship between an heir to a throne, who was abducted in an act of obedience to the will of God, and his rival for the throne. This heir knew he had a legal right, but he was guided by his moral obligation to righteousness (In the words of Spike Lee: "Do the Right Thing.") I am referring to David and Jonathan. For my none-reading bible folk, let me give you some background on this story before we go any further. In the Old Testament, we have Saul, who was anointed by the Prophet Samuel as the first king of the United Israel. The kingdom would later be divided into Israel in the north and Judah in the south. Saul would lose his reign and his descendants because of a series of, let's refer to as, "bad decisions". Jonathan was the legal heir to Saul's reign. Jonathan and David became best buds.

The book of 2 Samuel records in chapter 9, verses 1-13 that their friendship was for a lifetime and beyond.

This story is about David keeping a promise. In other words, David was determined to be a "Because Of" person. He showed his intentions by asking, after Johanthan death, "Is there still anyone left in the house of Saul to whom I may show kindness for Joathan's sake?" Daivd was told that there was a servant from the House of Saul, named Ziba, who would know. When Ziba came before Daivid, he told him that Joathan did have a son that was still alive. You would have thought this information was apt enough, but Ziba felt he needed to add that this son was "lame in both feet". You might think that this was just an attempt to illuminate the need for help from David. However, I can see that he stated this label as more than an announcement of need. His label was devaluing his worth. Why would I come to this conclusion you might ask? Because the answer is found in Jonathan's son's response to David's invitation of honor. In 2 Samuel, chapter 9, verse 5-8, we learn what happens when Jonathan's son was presented to the King:

5. Then King David sent and brought him from the house of Machir the son of Ammiel, at Lo-debar. 6 And Mephibosheth, the son of Jonathan, son of Saul, came to David and fell on his face and paid homage. And David said, "Mephibosheth!" And he answered, "Behold, I am your servant." 7 And David said to him, "Do not fear, for I will show you kindness for the sake of your father Jonathan, and I will restore to you all the land of Saul, father, and shall eat at my table always." 8 And he paid homage and said, "What is your servant, that you should show regard for a dog such as I?"

Did you see the scotoma that Mephibosheth had internalized because he had been labeled as a lame person? He was not just the last living child of Jonathan, he was a disabled child of Jonathan, which made him less than. This is a powerful illustration of what a person in power can do when they intentionally seek to be a "Because Of" person. King David had the power to wipe him out and kill him. What we instead see is the level of commitment King David had as a person. He was a man of integrity and loyalty. David only saw the son of his best friend, and not a dog or a "misfit" before him. This is the power of a "Because Of" person. They see not only the need, but the person's potential; they want to be a part of the birth of this potential and not the funeral.

According to the Jewish laws, Mephibosheth was still in the line for kingship. We also have a chance to witness the type of self-defeating, self-talk that takes place when we buy into our scotoma.

The system that is in place in America and around the world creates legal and socially accepted barriers to millions when they receive a medical diagnosis. In America, it happens in our school systems each year when children enroll. This process is in place to segregate students based on perceived learning needs. America has a propensity to use segregation principles to deal with anyone that is presented in a way that does not fit their preferred "type" of student. As we can see in the story of Mephibosheth, this is not a recent phenomenon.

It becomes even more insidious when race is added to the stigma of having a disability. To fully appreciate the challenges a person who has been labeled with a physical, developmental, or intellectual disability has in reaching their 100%, we must examine the "In Spite Of "terrain they must navigate.

Are you feeling me? Let us pause right here and confess that I am Mike Clinton Biggs Sr., and I was an "In Spite Of" person when it came to people with disabilities. I have been clean now for 23 years." When I was confronted with my condition, I responded like some people who are confronted about systemic racism. I pointed out that I had been working with people with disabilities since I was fifteen years old. I also pointed out that I, myself, was in special education when I was in school, so how could I possibly be an "In Spite Of" person? Some of my best friends have disabilities! This intervention through a situation with Person-Centered Planning (PCP) for a gentleman I was working with in a group home. Please understand, there is a lot to unpack around this event. This would serve as my second Born Again experience. I will refer to the person who was the center of this process as DB. It was my response to his needs being discussed that put a spotlight on my condition.

The result shed light on how I approach people with disabilities and the lens I viewed those people through. I was a senior at Troy State University. I was working part-time at the group home. My job title was… wait for it... "Houseparent"! There were four men in this home ranging from their twenties to their sixties. I was considered a "parent" to them. This title and distinction were my starting point for how and what services I was getting paid to provide. The woman that facilitated, Ruby Gray, was very well trained by the pioneers of PCP. (Side note: She would later become my wife. Stay with me, we are going somewhere!)

During DB's PCP, it became clear that I brought a medical model approach to how I viewed DB. In other words, I focused on his label/diagnosis. He had a sickness. He needed healing that could only be provided by professionals. DB just needed to follow our directions and then he would be all right. I was hostile about how much attention and resources they were wanting to give DB. I even mentioned my resentment of the fact that they have never offered my mother these types of services. At this point, Ruby had to remind me that we were here to plan for DB, and not my mother. That got my attention. After I picked myself up from that smackdown, I began to see how Ruby, as a facilitator, spoke of DB as a person and not as a patient or a client. The process presents a clinical social history by using a pictorial drawing of the focus person's life. Even the colors of the pens used have significance. It was clear that what was in BD's current Individual Service Plan (ISP) did not have anything to do with his empowerment and personhood. The system had decided what his 100% was, and up until this point, he had no say in the matter. I left this meeting feeling ashamed that I had been revealed as an "In Spite Of" person to people with disabilities. I had to do something about it. I saw how I demanded my rights as a person of color, but had not seen the discriminatory affect my role played on people with disabilities.

Through my participation in the process and my eventual embrace of PCP, my work did not go unnoticed. I had written papers on my experience with this new concept that had removed my scotoma to the needs of people who had been labeled and limited. DB was not healed, but he was given a life that he never imagined he could have. DB had changed me and many more because he was allowed to remove our scotoma's. DB gained what he had never had before; he could make his own choices. This was his 100%.

I was unable to attend seminary upon my graduation from Troy. One of my professors/mentors at Troy state, who at the time was the area director for the Mental Health/Mental Retardation/Developmental Disabilities/Substance Abuse program, offered me a job. The program he worked for is now referred to as the Division of Developmental Disabilities. An Area Director could waive required qualification for jobs if they found someone that they wanted on their team. The requirement for a masters was waived for me. Of course, this raised anger within the agency from those who thought they were more qualified. However, my qualifications were evidenced by the measurable improvements in people's lives.

This will help you understand why the services Chief, Gwen Martin, treated me the way she did on my first day on the job. She was holding a team meeting to introduce me to the other four center directors and the residential coordinator. They were all lined up in front of me in chairs. No one made eye contact with me. There was one other person of color on the team. I was smiling and so excited to be there, but this elation would disappear within the first ten minutes. This woman opened her mouth and said to me, "I will scrape you off my shoe like dog shit." She then said, "You mean nothing to me. I have thirty business cards for you because I do not see you making it through a 90-day probationary period." Wow. What had I gotten myself into? To reiterate, my selection to this position was controversial. Let me shed more light on this subject. When I was selected for this position, I was told to report to the Director of Developmental Services. This person managed the Early Intervention Program and Mental Retardation/Developmental Disabilities Services. (Mental Retardation was an accepted term in 1990 when I took this job. Thank God we have gotten rid of this label.) The complication was that this person had interviewed for the same position that my professor had been selected for. She had her team named and ready to go. She was not happy that she was not selected.

    I knew after the first meeting that I had better bring my A game!

    On this job, I came face to face with the intersection of racism and the suppression of rights for people labeled as disabled. I had six people assigned to receive services at the center I ran in South Georgia. They were, however, working at a plant away from the center. At this plant, they assembled water pumps. Most Americans are not aware that people with disabilities can be paid sub-minimum wages in some cases. This rate of pay is based on time studies that measure how long it takes a non-disabled individual to complete a task versus a disabled person to do the same task. These six individuals had worked there for six years and had not been reevaluated. The center also provided meals to the county jail for less than a reasonable value. In addition to these abuses, the center was $75,000.00 in the red. The consumers I served at that program never had a chance to reach their 100%. They had never been able to even imagine that they could seek any real vision for their lives.

    I took action to use the PCP (Person Centered Planning) approach to ensure they had a path to their 100%. It was not easy and would come at a cost. I had the six consumers time tested and the results showed that they were faster than the none-disabled workers. I told a very connected and powerful plant manager that they would not return until they are paid at the prevailing wage. They were removed from the plant for two months because of a decrease in revenue. They were rehired at the level of full pay. I did a cost comparison of meals we provided to the jail and found that we were providing the meals at 70% of the cost that other restaurants were charging. I raised the cost by 50% and was able to pay the consumers that worked in the kitchen minimum wage. This was a 120% increase to their income. I secured a contract for six of the ladies, who were trained quilt makers, at a clothing manufacturer for JCPenney. They were paid at 15% above minimum wage. I had the support of the Director who hired me, but not my immediate supervisor. The program went from $75,000.00 in the red to a $125,000.00 surplus.

The list of people whose lives reached their 100% were not only empowered by me, but many other people whose stories could fill this book. I want to fast forward this story and focus on a person I currently work with. He refused to accept his label/scotoma and reached his dream of becoming a radio broadcaster.

I have gotten permission to use his name. He is none other than Nate Chrisman; better known in the radio world as, "Nate the Great". I met Nate when I started my current job as a Pre-Employment Transition Specialist (PRE-EST). The company I work for is PQC. PQC has a contract, through the Indiana Department of Vocational Services, with the Jay County School System. I work with students that have Individual Education Plans or 504 Plans. These students have met requirements that provide accommodations for how they receive their education. The services I provide are through instruction, self- advocacy, job exploration, workforce readiness, post-secondary education, and work-based learning. I start my work with each child by doing an interview to get an idea of what career they would want to pursue when they graduate. Nate's interview can be seen on PQC Train's Facebook Page. Nate revealed in his interview that his desire is to be a radio announcer at WPGW, a local radio station. Nate talked about his Grandma Miller taking him there for the first time when he was ten years old. Nate said he spent the entire day asking questions and observing. It was at that point he decided he wanted to work there as a radio broadcaster.

Nate said he got a shortwave radio for Christmas and began to practice his skills. He set-up his own station with only a one-mile broadcast radius. Nate relayed to me that he has also recorded commercials at the station. After hearing his passion, my "Because Of" powers kicked in. The next day, I paid a visit to the owner of WPGW, Rob Weaver. I began to share my interview with Nate and ended the presentation by asking if Nate could shadow at the station to see if this was really what he wanted to do. Unbeknownst to me, Nate had made quite the impression on Rob. Rob went beyond my request and offered the Saturday, 5 PM to 9 PM, spot to Nate. Rob disclosed to me that he was not sure Nate could handle it, but was willing to try it regardless. I had found another "Because Of" person: Mr. Rob Weaver.

    Getting Nate the job so fast created some logistical issues. I had to get permission to provide Nate PRE-EST services while he was on the job. I had to commit to working with Nate on Saturday nights. This ended up being a seven-month commitment. At that point, I was working seven days a week. I work at a group home on the weekends. I would leave the group home and drive an hour to pick Nate up. Then, after dropping him home, I would drive an hour back to the group home. I cannot overstate that "Because Of" people go the extra mile if needed. They understand that, if you can, you must do things that genuinely help people on their path to 100%. "In Spite Of" people demand that you must pull yourself up by your bootstraps, even if you are barefoot!

How is Nate doing, you might be wondering? Well, not only has Nate mastered the operations involved in broadcasting, but he has also become a studio producer. These duties ensure that when other broadcasters are doing a remote broadcast, they stay on air. Nate has worked several broadcasts by himself. Nate's success has opened the eyes of his community on what is possible when they stop looking at labels and look at the person.

CHAPTER 5
WHAT IS THE SECRET TO FINDING YOUR 100%?

    My goal in authoring this book is to provide a clear overview of the struggles in making the most of the life we have each been given. My attempt is to not paint a rosy picture of what we face alone this journey. Even those who have been born into privilege have challenges in defining who they are and reaching their 100%. Therefore, here is the secret: your 100% is not a destination, but a process. This is critical for the reader to understand. There is no silver bullet or magical formula. It is a process that is brightened by the presence of "Because Of" people, and at times, fueled by overcoming "In Spite Of" people. It involves the pain of discovering and removing scotomas. The destinations sometimes are mountain tops and sometimes they are valleys. Your 100% is not the end point, but is the energy you have to press on. For someone like me, it is powered by my faith in Jesus. For others, it is just determination. Whatever your source of inspiration may be, use it.

Please don't think of this as a "How To" book, but rather a "Why I Should" book. I have written how my faith has been tried while authoring this book. It has been shaken by events that are out of my control and are affecting the entire world, as we learn to live with Covid 19. The prevention of its spread has been politicized in America, among other places in the world. This politicization is causing it to spread and many to needlessly die. I have seen over half of America buy into this dangerous and potentially deadly mistake. It caused me to question, "What is the point in authoring a book about a process that demands you to push through in the presence of 'In Spite Of' people or in the absence of 'Because Of' people." I found my answer in my question. At what time in the world has obedience been so necessary, (besides the Garden of Eden)? Each generation has always had groups who had to face the fact that life is not fair. People had to choose to fight for their 100%. So, our current place in history is not only demanding change, but seeing it through.

Therefore, if we start with the supposition that finding your 100% is a process and not a destination, then it is logical that we must master the process. To master the process, we need a formula. Here is my attempt to provided one:

Process: Reality + Determination x Support-Obstacles = your 100%

Let me break down each component. This formula takes

in consideration that each individual faces different challenges, but the end result can be grouped in this manner regardless of the individual's situation.

I. Reality Phase

This is the most critical phase in the process. We have discussed and provided examples of how we form our self-image and/or view our abilities. We have discussed the role of scotomas. Scotomas serve as blinders to our abilities and potential. They are at work consciously and unconsciously in our lives. They are the most powerful forces that hinder us in finding our 100%. We must identify them and reorganize our reality of who we are and what our potential is. This is an exceedingly difficult part of the journey. During this discovery, we must face the damage that "In Spite Of" people, who might be family, friends, church members, leaders, and even our educators, may have knowingly and unknowingly afflicted on us.

I want to give a personal example of how damage is done unknowingly. I am the same height now that I was at age twelve. Six feet and one inch tall. I had a full beard by that time. Therefore, I went through puberty at a much earlier age than my classmates. When I was twelve, my mother, grandmother, and cousins had gathered in the kitchen with the window open. I was outside playing with friends my age and younger. I was acting my age, but not my shoe size. The ball had rolled under the window, and they did not see me come to retrieve it. I heard my beloved grandmother say, "Y'all see how Mike is playing out there... They say you can outgrow your senses." Because I was self-conscious about my size, this stung me to my core. I am sure my grandmother would not have intentionally hurt me. Her love was always present. The only thing I thought I could do to show I had grown up was to start smoking and hanging out with the older guys. This was my choice. Was it wise? Absolutely not. But at this point in my life, I did not understand self-destructive behavior.

    I would like to turn our focus to David of the Bible again. David is presented in the Bible as someone with both strengths and weaknesses. In other words, a human being! He has successes and failures. He finds himself struggling to figure out the "why" and not the "how". Why is it so difficult to seek his 100%? Why does a loving God abandon him and allow the "In Spite Of" people to torment him? Let us look at one of the most challenging moments he faced in coming to terms with this reality.

    In 1 Samuel 22:1-2, we find David in a cave named Adullam. He is seeking refuge from King Saul, as he has come to see David as a threat. David's fame had even reached the King of Gath. He asked King Achish for sanctuary before he went to the cave. However, this King echoed King Saul's fear of David. In 1 Sam 21:11, he asked David, "Is not this David the king of the land? Did they not sing one to another of him in dances saying 'Saul hath slain his thousands, and David his ten thousand?'" When David heard this, he knew it would not end well. So, he started to act as if he had a mental condition. King Achish believed David's deception and let him go.

So, David found his home in Adullam. What is striking about this, is that Adullam, when translated, means refuge. This cave was located not too far from the battlefield where David had killed Goliath. We do not know how long he was in this cave, but we do have a record of some of his thoughts while he was in the cave. We find them in Psalm 142:

142 I cried unto the Lord with my voice; with my voice unto the Lord did I make my supplication.
2 I poured out my complaint before him; I shewed before him my trouble.
3 When my spirit was overwhelmed within me, then thou knewest my path. In the way wherein I walked have they privily laid a snare for me.
4 I looked on my right hand, and beheld, but there was no man that would know me: refuge failed me; no man cared for my soul.
5 I cried unto thee, O Lord: I said, Thou art my refuge and my portion in the land of the living.
6 Attend unto my cry; for I am brought very low: deliver me from my persecutors; for they are stronger than I.
7 Bring my soul out of prison, that I may praise thy name: the righteous shall compass me about; for thou shalt deal bountifully with me.
KJV

We do not know how long it was between this Psalm and when his "Because Of" people found him. But we know he had to find his "why", so he could continue his fight. The reality phase is where we must face our fears and faith. This is where we must decide if the juice is worth the squeeze. Many like to rush through this process by declaring a victory scripture or getting anointed with oil. I am sure for some; this has its place. However, for many, it should not be rushed. For those who are not believers, if you rush through this by declaring your power, preparation, and persistence, you may fail under the relentless challenges life will throw at you. David had done everything right. Yet, he endured hatred and resentment from his king. His family and he were fleeing for their lives. The "In Spite Of" people do not give up easily. In our time, they may try to shade you on social media. They may email your new employer, significant other, and even your children. The damage could seem insurmountable. However, this is where you need your own cave to seek refuge in and find out what you are made of. This is where, if you are a believer, you decide you can trust faith. If you are not a believer, this is where you show your refusal to fail.

In the military, we have a phrase for finding appreciation in the challenges that are physical and mental. We say, "Embrace the Suck." The Suck cannot be avoided, it must be addressed if you want to get to your 100%. Nothing and no one will protect you from it, but you can find the help to go through it. This is where you must come to terms with your limitations and abilities.

II. The Determination Phase

This phase naturally follows the Reality Phase. You have accessed what you can change and what you cannot change. You know what you must do now to continue the 100% journey. However, I would like to point out some pitfalls you could face in this process. The number one challenge is: unrealistic goal setting. What do I mean by this? I mean that you can run the risk of overestimating or underestimating your abilities. I was told a story once about a man and his son who had to cut the grass in their fields. They did not have a "ride behind" mower. All they had was a sling blade. (Okay millennials, please get your Google Machine out and search "sling blade". I will wait for you. Now, back to the story.) The son wanted to show his father how strong he was and just went to town on the grass. The father took his time and would stop ever so often to sharpen his blade. By the end of the day, the father had cut just as much grass and was not as tired. The point of this story is speed should not be the goal. You must look for quality over quantity. Determination must have an assessment plan. Determination plus assessment prevents burnout and failure. You can be determined to get to a location, but if you have not figured out the best route, you could make a lot of bad turns. For my believers, determination is not repeating scripture and the most popular Christian catchphrases of the day. It is taking that class you need to get the job or promotion you want. It is seeking counseling to address what you are doing to hinder your relationship. It could be starting an exercise program to ensure you have a healthy life. It may mean changing your schedule to have more time with your children. Determination without a plan is a promise, not a commitment.

III. Support Phase

If you have properly navigated the other two phases, you should have come to the realization you cannot reach your 100% alone. Even for the believer, you must understand that just faith in God is not enough. Let me explain, before I do more damage to my believer status. What I mean by this is that God places people in our lives to complete his plans for us. Dr. Bobby Clark said that "a Christian will receive assurance from God on the destination of their 100% by one of two ways. It will come by double confirmation or a creeping vine experience". A double confirmation is when two different people confirm the 100% and its destination in your life. This may be in the form of confirming a career choice you were thinking of or what city you were moving to. The plan you have produced in the determination phase will sometimes have an outside confirmation.

The creeping vine experience is different. It happens in a less direct way. It is not hearing a word from someone, but a culmination of an event or situation that leads you to your destination. It could appear as random events or chance meetings. But when they come together, they give you the confidence you need to move forward.

It does not matter which way got you to this point. What matters is that your "Because Of" people, or person, is ready to help empower you on your journey. We talked about Daivd having to find refuge in a cave. While he was in the cave, he found out that he had four hundred "Because Of" men, who were willing to fight for him and even die for him. They came to the cave to be with him as he worked through his understanding of his 100%. Even David knew he would need help to reach his 100%. He never said, "All I need is God. You can just leave me here in the cave and God will deliver me!" No, God recognizes the work we put in. He works through our "Because Of" people and guides us around our "In Spite Of" people. Therefore, David had a creeping vine experience. The four hundred did not all show up at the same time. As they came, he could recognize God at work in his life. He gained confidence in how he could survive the hatred of an "In Spite Of" king.

Your support team will assemble when you have put in the work. Your work and commitment will draw to you what you need to succeed. They will find you. You may find that it is the people you did not even suspect noticed you. It appears to be what non-believers call "serendipity". But, make no mistake, your support will come when you recognize your need for it.

IV. Obstacles

I have tried to stress throughout this book that finding your 100% is not easy. The world does not operate on the principle of making sure everything is fair and square. We know that there is always a war around us, constantly being fought by "Because Of" people and "In Spite Of" people. Sometimes, you are not even present and participating. Someone could be speaking unkindly about you, and a "Because Of" person could be there to set the record straight and you never know it happened. Or, someone could be out to do harm to you and circumstances could prevent them from following through on their intent.

I remember when I was in the Army, I had one of those experiences. It was the only time I was not serving on a LB Team. (LB Team is what Preventive Medicine Detachment was called when I was on active duty. Our mission was much larger than our description. Trust me). I was the only Preventive Medicine Specialist in the 1,600 person I97th Infantry Brigade, in FT Benning, GA. We had a new company commander; Captain Paul was the most difficult "In Spite Of" person I had ever dealt with while I was in the Army. I was assigned to the medic unit, Bravo Company, which he commanded. To this day, I am not sure why he hated me, but I do know what I did to make him hate me more. My assignment before I got to the 197th was with the 71st LB Team in Grafenwoehr, Germany. I could author a book by itself on this team and its mission, but I am going to give you the condensed version. In the Army, your job is called "Military Occupation Specialty Code", or MOS for short. My MOS was a 91S (it has now been changed to 68S) Preventive Medicine Tech. When I first joined the Army, the 91S MOS was just reactivated. They had closed it at the end of the Vietnam War. There were less than six hundred and fifty of us serving when I came in. You would leave that job after you made Sergeant E-5.

The Army began to recognize their need to keep us in our job. This is due in large part to the work put in by LB Teams, as well as LC Teams. We were designed for facing things, like the Covid pandemic we are in now for example. The 71st LB Team had a 1st Sergeant position. This position is normally filled by an E-8 or an E-7 promotable Sergeant. By 1980, we could stay in this MOS up to E-6. There were no E-8 91S's to hold 1st SGT potions. Therefore, as an E-5, I held a 1st SGT position. I also would hold command time. When I was on LB Teams, we only had eight people per team. There was only one officer and he or she was the commander. If there was no commander, the 1st SGT became the commander until it was filled by an officer. I had the opportunity twice as a Non-Commissioned Officer to hold command. This allowed me to attend the Commanders/1st SGT as an E-5. I know of only two others who also had this opportunity, Larry Fain and Kim Kanost.

Captain Paul was aware of my background and was not impressed, but rather felt threatened for some reason. He began to harass me. He gave me a counseling statement for not scoring 100% on the skills qualification test (SQT). This is an annual required test the Army would give to ensure you were qualified for your MOS. You only had to score 60% to remain qualified. My score dropped to a 94. Less than 1% of the Army has ever scored 100% and "Special Education Mike" did it twice! The next event sealed my fate with him. Captain Paul had recommended disciplinary action against a friend of mine, called an Article 15. If it was successful, he was facing a reduction in rake and forfeiture of pay. Because I had attended the Commanders/1st SGT academy, I knew how to help him defeat it. He took my advice and won. The word got back to Captain Paul and he was "38" Hot!

 I did not know he had an officer spying on me until he threatened to file charges of dereliction of duties on me with Captain Paul. The office watched me do an inspection, which was not complete. I did not do a complete inspection because the SGT had failed to come to my required class. This was before cell phones. When the officer got back to his unit, he had an emergency call from the hospital stating his wife and kids had been in a wreck. He never got a chance to talk with Captain Paul, because we had to deploy to Ft. Irwin, California. I would come back to Ft. Benning and be transferred to Korea before they could talk.

 What was the point of this story? Your successes will not protect you from obstacles. You will never be safe from the hinders that "In Spite Of" people will throw your way or life changing events.

 Here is a break in my story. I've encountered the most painful event that will force me to put everything I just wrote into practice. I know this needs to be added.

 Within two days of writing the above section in my book, I got a call from my son, Mike Jr. He had noticed blood in his stool. Because his mother had colon cancer, I begged him to get checked by a doctor and he did. He had to have a biopsy and it required a more difficult procedure.

Before I go any further, I need to add some back-story for clarification. Mike Jr. had a gastroschisis birth defect. His organs, except his heart and lungs, were on the outside of his body. This means his stomach walls did not form and were left open. Mike's birth was the first one I had ever witnessed. I was not aware of what was going on. I thought they had damaged my wife, Delores, during the delivery. Mike was born at Martin Army Hospital, in Ft Benning, GA. After his birth, I heard the doctor say, "Call Dr. Starr and Goldman. Prepare him to be transported to the NICU Unit at the Medical Center of Columbus, GA." I would soon learn how this call would save my son's life. This was forty-two years ago, on April 10, 1978. I could not see the bigger picture at the time, but I had switched assignments with a person who I went to basic training with, named Clarence Dipisa. I had orders for the embassy in London after I finished Advanced Individual Training at Ft. Sam, Houston, TX. Dipisa had orders for Ft. Benning. Dipisa had family in London, and I was born in Columbus. We switched. This assignment put me thirty miles from where I was raised in Talbotton, GA. God had a bigger plan.

    Dr. Starr and Goldman were two of the leading experts in gastroschisis birth defects. They taught at Emory University. They pioneered treatments that increased the survival rates for these rare births. However, when I got to the NICU Unit at the Medical Center, I discovered that there were twelve other babies being treated for the same issue as Mike. I was met by a social worker, who told me to "take a picture of Mike, because he may not be alive when I come back" because I was going back to Martin

Army to see Delores. I boldly declared, "He will be alive when I return. He is flesh of my flesh and blood of my blood. My first-born son and God have him."

I rushed back to Martin Army and told Delores what was happening. She would have to spend two more weeks there recovering from Preeclampsia. I thank God I was living so close to my family. My mother, Biese and my grandmother, Lillian, sprang into action and provided care to Danyiell, my 4-year-old daughter, while I lived between the two hospitals.

The hardest part of this was bonding with the other parents who had a child with the same birth defect. We started with twelve babies, and by the tenth week after Mike was born, there were only two still living. Adam Parker's son, Mike, and my son, Mike. Adam was a member of the Columbus Fire Department. We bonded fast. We still stay in contact to this day. We are both so thankful for Dr. Starr and Goldman and all the nurses of the Medical Center's NICU unit.

Forty-two years later, and my faith is just as strong now as the doctors tell me my oldest son, Mike Jr, has been diagnosed with Stage 4 Small Intestinal cancer on November 6, 2020. My trust in him has not changed. Mike had to have eleven major operations before he was five years old, and God brought him through. His life is in God's hands and in the hands of the great doctors working at St. Elizabeth in Florence, KY.

Another chapter in keeping my 100% is unfolding. I have had to resign from Jay County Jr/Sr High School. I am in the process of finding a place to live for Mike and myself in Kentucky. I must find a job that I can schedule around meeting his needs. Make no mistake, it is challenging, but I am prepared to find my "Because Of" team. My brother, Darryl, is two hours away, my sister, Ann, is on speed dial, and my brother, Ronnie, is praying. My daughter, Danyiell, and sons, Gabrial and Miguel, are on deck. Mike Jr's daughter, Enailah, is standing strong. My favorite cousin, Denise Perryman, was the first to send financial help. I also had a co-worker, Virginia Richardson, send a love offering. The students and staff of Jay County Jr/Sr High School gave me a great going away party that included gifts, cards, and cash.

    The Brighton Center lived up to their motto: "Once Brighton Center Always Brighton Center". Mike's rent was due. As a graduate of Brighton's Center for Employment Training, he was able to apply for and get rental assistance. They cut a check for $500.00. I can say without a doubt that this is one of the best nonprofits in America. I was the Financial Aid Coordinator and a Success Coach at the Center for Employment Training where Mike got his certification in Business Computer Technology. It was one of his proudest accomplishments.

    It is times like this that has compelled me to author this book. I want those who read this not to be crushed by the last part of the process in finding their 100%. Things will happen that you have absolutely no control over, which will encourage you to quit or lose your faith. But, you can withstand the tough times if you understand it is part of the life cycle that we must learn to navigate. We must not see it as an enemy. It is part of the process that teaches us how to grow in our faith and abilities. This phase of the process gives us the ability to expand our "Because Of" network "and resilience. It also robs "In Spite Of" people and negative situations of their victories.

It has taken me three months to process Mike Jr's end of life journey. Now, I can write about it.

I am just now able to return to authoring this book. The previous passages are the last things I wrote after getting Mike Jr's diagnosis. I was in a state of optimism. Mike Jr. passed away on December 13th. It was a roller coaster of events and emotions. Mike's cancer had progressed more than the doctors had initially thought. After the last biopsy, they determined the cancer had spread to his kidneys and his lungs. The doctor's thought chemotherapy was an option. We went through the training on what to expect. We discussed the pros and cons and decided on the treatment. However, he was not able to eat after Thanksgiving. A feeding tube was ruled out. He could only get nourishment through drinking Ensure and juices. I went to every store in Kentucky and Cincinnati trying to find 350grams of Strawberry Ensure; this was Mike Jr's favorite. But, it was to no avail. Thank God Mike's Landlord, Sherri Williard's daughter ordered two cases from Amazon. This would not be the only act of support we would receive from them. Unfortunately, he was only able to drink two bottles before he had his procedure. He had to have a G-tube inserted to drain the fluids. The G-tube was not without consequences, as it had to be re-inserted twice and clogged frequently. I remained by his bedside to keep it cleaned and flowing. Due to a lack of nutrition, Mike began to grow weaker. We both came to accept that death was drawing near.

My birthday would come on the 5th of December. Just eight days before he would pass. I was at my lowest point. I wondered why God was letting me see another birthday, when Mike Jr. may not reach his. I truly had little rest. I only left his bedside to take a bath and handle any business we had that I could not do by phone. My youngest grand girl, at the time, MaKenna (A.K.A. Jellybean), FaceTime me every day. She put together a Birthday surprise for me and a visit to her uncle, Mike Jr. However, Mike Jr did not want anyone to see his weight loss. I did not push the subject. I managed with the help and support of my daughter-in-law, Amber Biggs. They baked a cake, brought cards, gifts, and bought tickets for us to visit the Newport Aquarium, the day after my birthday. I will never forget this act of love and concern; I needed this respite for what lay ahead. My grandkids would be a major part of my support throughout this part of the journey.

The last three days of his life involved him reflecting on his faith, life, and failures. We processed both our lives with laughter and tears. Mike had a chance to contact many in his life to set things right with and to give his thanks. This process was full of challenges. Mike Jr. had renounced the faith his mom and I had raised him in. However, I was determined to ensure that this situation was not going to turn me into an "In Spite Of" father in his eyes. Wisdom had taught me that this was not the time for theological debt. I was not there to be his pastor or his evangelist; I was there to be his father. I trusted God to do that in better ways than I could. To evangelistic minded Christians, this might seem like a copout. "What if he died before you witnessed to him"? "You have an obligation to share the Word when a person is facing death". "Oh contriver"! I have an obligation to live my witness and share only when the Holy Spirit says it's time. Issues that Mike and I had, concerning religion and some events in his life, would be resolved by one of his faith leaders. She helped him to understand how his attacks on my faith had gone overboard. She provided him with recordings that he and he alone should hear and not be used to attack my faith. Death and dying is a subject that Christians are not always good at handling. We are so quick to invoke the name of Jesus and declare an outcome of our choosing. Death is one of the most powerful situations that can derail our pursuit of our 100%. I am extremely fortunate to have faced this issue while seeking my master's in biblical counseling. I had no idea that I would need a paper I wrote in 2017 to get me through Mike Jr's death. I was given an assignment to review C.S. Lewis's *A Grief Observed* in the form of a letter. I would like to share it with you. In it, I discuss how we all have diverse backgrounds but found our commonality in facing the death of a loved one. I talk about how death challenges your faith and can cause you to feel an intense anger at God, others, and yourself. Here is the letter I wrote:

Mike Biggs

A Letter to C.S. Lewis

Dear C.S.,

I hope you do not mind me addressing you as C.S. This is not an attempt to show any disrespect to a man of your standing and stature. It is my way of introducing my new feelings of solidarity and the respect I have for you. Specifically, your very personal book "A Grief Observed." Although I have been academically acquainted with you, beginning in the eighties, it was a very distant acquaintance. I found you both too high brow and very culturally distant from my world.

However, after reading A Grief Observed at age fifty-nine, it has been so much different in how I see you. How might you ask? Well, I share the loss of a wife to cancer. I have lost not only the love of my life, but the mother of my children. My marriage to her also caused some heads to turn in my church and family. Unlike you being fifteen years older than H, Delores was seven years older than I. She also had a three-year-old daughter I would go on to adopt and make a part of my life. Our bond is as strong as the ones I have with my three biological sons. I shared an immensely powerful anger at God for allowing her to get sick and die. I, as you, could not be comforted with my theological understanding of the role of suffering. Also, I confused my suffering with Delores's suffering. My needs with her needs. Wanting to change places with her.

However, my anger was not only at God, but her, also. She had managed to keep knowledge of her cancer *from both me and the children. She held to her belief in divine healing until the end. Why did she not seek medical care? How could she have hidden the pain she was in from us? Why did I stay on the road so much? How could a loving God let this happen? I also journaled about this dark place. It was another level of grief that I felt God placed on me for no apparent reason. How different from me was your experience with journaling? My journaling did not end my grief. I was stuck and did not know.*

But my friend, like you, I could not abandon the truth that God is my God. Jesus is my savior. My faith brought me healing from the reeling. It is not to say I still do not have my moments, as I am sure you did. When a new grandchild is born that she will ever see... Or when our children are facing life's challenges that I know her insight would be of much more value, I grave. Nevertheless, my fear and anger melts with the rays of proven love God has provided me. I am now able to walk with others on their grief journey. I know the power of "the walk without the talk..."

Thank you, my friend, for showing me that death is an equalizer. That education, power, or position cannot shield us from facing grief.

Your Brother in Christ

Mike Biggs

When I write about being prepared for any unforeseen circumstance or situations, the most devastating and challenging ones are:

1. Sexual Trauma
2. Death of a loved one.

I can only speak in the first-person concerning death. I am not a victim of sexual trauma. However, both have the same process for moving forward. Grief, anger, and forgiveness are all a part of healing. There is no "same size fits all" approach to resolving any of these stages. I am a firm believer in the need of having a great counselor or spiritual leader who can walk with you on this path. Notice I said walk "with you". Please be careful of those who come with a prescription that tells you how and when to do the things that may have worked for them. Remember, everyone's 100% is different. That is not to say that new techniques must be developed for anyone facing these traumas. However, duration and sequencing of what methods and techniques work in the healing process is totally individualized. I have been fortunate to return to my VA Counselor in Cincinnati. Her name is Dr. Meredith Clump. I am extremely hard on counselors, because education has been given more credibility than effectiveness in bringing people into the field. I became a Community Mental Health Counselor in 1990 with a bachelor's degree. I worked under the supervision of a license councilor. I was just as effective or sometimes more effective than many of my licensed co-workers. I brought years of pastoral counseling to the table. I have had to put all the processes of finding your 100% to use in real time in dealing with my son's cancer and eventual death. The greatest support I received was from my old counselor, Dr. Meredith Clump. I first met Dr. Clump when I was being treated for PTSD at the Ft. Thomas V.A. Domiciliary. Dr. Clump works with Dr. Katie Chard, Director of the PTSD and Anxiety Disorders Division for the Cincinnati V.A. I can say without a doubt this is the best program in the VA system. It changed and saved my life. Because I am a counselor, I am extremely hard on this profession. Mainly, because of the damage that can be done to hurting people. This program exceeds my expectations.

 Dr. Clump helped guide me through the self-examination process. During Mike Jr's transition, there were times when I wanted to beat myself up for my failures as a father. Mike Jr. shared with me several traumatic events he had been through while I was on deployment; things I had no idea he had experienced. I would sometimes think that I was not doing enough to help him with his cancer. Because Dr. Clump knew me so well, she was able to remind me of the scotomas we had dealt with in our previous counseling sessions. Not only was she a part of my self-examination, but she was also a part of my "Because Of" support team.

 Through her walk with me along Mike Jr's illness and death, I was able to be with him in the moment. I did not feel I had to be in control. I allowed him to dictate the subjects of conversation. I would raise conversations around moments of joy we had shared and let him lead where we would go next. Without asking, Mike Jr. would assure me that he "thanked God he had me as a father". He was so appreciative that I was always there when he needed me. He thanked me for bringing him to the Center of Employment Training, ensuring he had a debt free education. He said he appreciated how I tended to his business for him. For two days, we sat in silence as he reflected on his impending death. The last words he spoke to me were, "Dad all those revivals you, Rev. Robinson, and Rev. Baker preached has prepared me for this."

Trust me, I am looking back on these moments and only now am I able to fully process what happened. There were so many things I had to work on before his transition. I had no time to process. I was told I could bring Mike home for hospice. I had to pull a lot of strings to get a place for him to come. I called my friend, Dan Claire of the DAV, and declared I was homeless to get emergency housing through the VA. By the grace of God, I had a lot of "Because Of" people in the VA emergency housing programs in Cincinnati. I was able to get a furnished, all utilities included apartment from the Talbert House. I was able to move in on Thanksgiving. I will never forget Julie Roberts, Case Manager at Talbert House's Health Care for Homeless Veterans Program. She came in on her day off to check me in. I was only fifteen minutes from Mike Jr. I needed this apartment because the room he rented would not have accommodated his hospital bed. Also, Mike Jr was boarding and there was not a place for me. Most importantly, I had no income.

During Mike Jr's illness, I had to take extreme

precautions in ensuring I did not bring the Covid infection to him; I feared that the most. I masked and washed my hands whenever I went out to take care of business or get something to eat. I lived in fear of making his health even worse if I failed to take necessary precautions. Covid loomed over this entire process like a lion stalking its prey. It impacted every decision I made. I thank God that the Covid protocols did not prevent me from being with my son during his transition. The last three days of Mike Jr's life was nothing short of a roller coaster of difficulties.

    I got the final approval to bring him to my transition apartment for hospice on his last Friday. I met with the hospice team to finalize the plan on that Friday at noon. Mike was talking and able to participate in the discussions. However, by 2 P.M., he was in pain and needed injectable pain meds. This, I thought, was just a slight interruption to him coming home with me. That would not be the case. By 10 P.M., he would stop being able to talk. His pain was increasing. I could see him slipping away. The last conversation I had with him, he told me something I will cherish the rest of my life. He said, "Dad I am so thankful I have you as a father. A living representation of my Heavenly Father." I will hold on to those words as I would anything that could have value attached to it.

    The nurse on duty at the Blue Ash Cincinnati Hospice House where Mike Jr. passed was Jamie Ehrlich. Jamie was an angel. She prepared me for what to expect in Mike's last hours. I monitored and kept his G-tub cleaned and she managed his pain. I was the only person in the room when Mike Jr. took his last breaths at 2:30 P.M.,

December 13, 2020. I went to get her and she called his time of death. Mike had a "Do Not Resuscitate" order in place. He said he did not want me to go through what I, and the family, went through during his mother's battle with cancer. He went peacefully with care and dignity.

My Sister, Angela, ensured that I did not have to worry about the funeral costs. Per usual, she was there for me. She took the weight of the world off my shoulders. Her generosity allowed me to focus on getting Mike back to Talbotton to be laid to rest. I am so glad to have a sister that is one of my "Because Of" people. I have always been able to count on her support.

Covid would make its presence known again. Because of all the deaths related to Covid, there was a backlog for getting services from the local funeral homes. Nurse Jamie knew I was overwhelmed at this time. Mike's brothers, the twins, Gabriel and Miguel, were enroute, but had not arrived in time to be with their brother and me. Nurse Jamie sprang into action and told me she would make the arrangements to get his body picked up. It would be 6:30 P.M. before she got a confirmation and 8:30 PM before they came to get his body. Miguel and Gab arrived during this time and were a big support for me.

Covid would continue to impose its will on the process of finding my 100%. Even after securing the services of Walker Funeral Home, it would be over a week before they could do the cremation. There was another backlog due to Covid deaths. I was in agony just thinking about not being able to put him to rest. I was also told I would lose my apartment if I left to take him home for burial. The VA Housing program required me to sign in every morning. It would be December 26th before I could pick up his remains. I scheduled his graveside funeral, Monday the 28th. I have no regrets for having to manipulate the rules to get him home to Talbotton to be buried next to my mother, as he requested. Because of Covid, the service would have to be graveside. Shawnna Preston, someone I have had a special relationship with for the last 10 years, would open her home to me and Enailah.

    Shawnna is one of my "Because Of" people. She is the reason I am pursuing my 100% VA Disability. Shawnna was with me when I went to a hearing concerning the denial of my claim. She was there when I was told that my "records were permanently and indefinitely sealed". I was told this was because of the sensitivity of my missions. I was devastated and I was ready to give up. Shawnna was not having any of it. The VA Rep, after Shawnna demanded to know how I could get around this, told me how I could fight it. I am not at liberty to discuss the issue or the missions I was on, currently. I hope I will be able to in the future.

    Shawnna, SISI "My Pizza Pie" (Shawnna's granddaughter, who I also love as a granddaughter), and my big brother, Ronnie, would clean off the cemetery that Sunday. Enailah had never met her ancestors that were buried on Smith Hill in our family plot. I took this time to give her a family history. She was so excited.

    I took Mike's ashes by all the places that meant so much to him. We had a private procession. I took him to the places he had lived, we drove by the Medical

Center where he was treated at birth, we drove by Rose's Caribbean Restaurant, and Canon Brewery, where he had highlighted his cooking skills, and finally we went by his mother's grave. It was one of the most emotional drives I had ever taken. He shared my love of history and I know this was the best way to honor his life.

On December 28, at 2 P.M., we celebrated Mike's home-going. It was a perfect day for a graveside service. The sun was out and not a cloud in the sky. I was assisted in the service by Rev. Jennett Pinkston, my childhood friend for life, and my cousin Rev. Alfred Biggs, (A.K.A Al Bubba). My Cousin/Brother, Greg Grice, and Elnor did the obituary and video of the service. It was truly a time of celebrating Mike's life. Danyiell and Miguel with their families were there. My favorite Cousin, Dennis Perryman, Shawnna's daughter, Nisha, and her nephew Carvall, had set-up the repass. Covid may have diminished the size of his home-going, but not the quality. Quality over quantity, always. I am attaching a video link of the service in the index.

Sally and LeBron Fergerson would provide financial support for my travel cost. Sally was the Chairwoman of the Talbot County School Board when I started the Talbot County Alternative Charter Academy. She never wavered in her support of me, regardless of the political pressure she faced. The Fergusons were role models for many of us. They produced the current mayor of Talbotton, GA, Tony Lamar, and Dr. Terry Fergerson, one of the stars of the hit show, *Critter Fixers*.

After the services, everything went blurry. I had

limited time to spend with my grandchildren, Daniel, Liberty, Miguel Jr, and Mikie. Nevertheless, I enjoyed their support. I must say I was feeling some kind of way because Miguel is six foot seven and Mikie is six foot four... I am no longer the tallest. Gabriel and his kids could not attend. They were missed. Gabriel's daughter, Amarri, along with Miguel Jr and Mikie had spent more time together than any of my other grandchildren. I had only four hours of rest before I had to drop Enailah back home and return to Cincinnati. Enailah and I would have one more bonding moment on the way home. As we approached the Jackson-Hartsfield Airport, Enailah spotted my DAV Victory for Veterans Billboard. Enailah screamed, 'Granddad, that's you up there!' I never felt as proud of being on a billboard as I did at that moment. It was an enormously proud moment for me.

I dropped off Enailah and headed back to Cincinnati to sign-in before 9AM. I was very tired and emotionally drained. I took solace in knowing I had laid Mike to rest on Smith Hill next to my mom, as he requested. I did not have time to grieve. My focus was on handling business. It has been an ongoing process. At times, I could not bring myself to write about these events. At other times, I found myself crying uncontrollably. However, now I find myself reflecting on the things he did that made me smile.

  The point of all the stories I just shared is: life is unpredictable. It will always throw a curveball at you. You never reach a point in life where you are free from facing unforeseen obstacles and barriers to reaching your 100%.

However, when you have a system in place to respond to, you overcome and continue the mission. I had to follow this process of:

Reality + Determination x Support-Obstacles = your 100%

I had to get back on the path to my 100% at age 62. I did not return to work for PQC after Mike Jr's death. I took a job in Kentucky working with veterans and quickly discovered that there were too many triggers that reminded me of his death and suffering. I moved back to Union City with my brother, Darryl. Within a month, I was presented with an opportunity to be in a new program as a School Credit Recovery Coach. I would help students who had fallen behind during the Covid pandemic. I am a part of a team that is developing an academic and employment program. I get to work within the skill sets that I have mastered. My job will be to ensure the students I serve will be able to graduate and pick a career they would like to pursue. I have no idea where this job will take me, but I know I am on the path of elevating my 100% in my golden years.

CONCLUSION

I authored this book with the intent to present a framework to process life events that either propel us or hinder us in seeking our 100%. Finding your 100% is a process and not a destination. It allows for the reality that we cannot control all negative events that come in our lifetimes. However, we have a process we use to respond to them. This is the challenge: dealing with life when it is not fair. When we attach accomplishment to the idea that they will shield us from pain, we have set ourselves up for crippling disappointment. We end up in the depressive, self-talk that asks, "Why me?" We start questioning our actions that may have caused the problem. Unrealistic expectations are where faith and hope go to die. We can come to the conclusion that we are "doomed to defect".

It is critical that we have a worldview that sees beyond the things we have no control over. We all have scotomas that block our view of what we are truly capable of accomplishing. We, most times, do not know how much

Conclusion

they affect us until we are presented with opportunities to reach our 100%. Let us look at how Moses' scotoma affected him. In Exodus 4: 10-16, Moses attempts to talk God into believing he was not the leader God thought he was.

10 Moses said to the LORD, "Pardon your servant, Lord. I have never been eloquent, neither in the past nor since you have spoken to your servant. I am slow of speech and tongue."
11 The LORD said to him, "Who gave human beings their mouths? Who makes them deaf or mute? Who gives them sight or makes them blind? Is it not I, the LORD? 12 Now go; I will help you speak and will teach you what to say."
13 But Moses said, "Pardon your servant, Lord. Please send someone else."
14 Then the LORD's anger burned against Moses, and he said, "What about your brother, Aaron the Levite? I know he can speak well. He is already on his way to meet you, and he will be glad to see you. 15 You shall speak to him and put words in his mouth; I will help both of you speak and will teach you what to do. 16 He will speak to the people for you, and it will be as if he were your mouth and as if you were God to him. 17 But take this staff in your hand so you can perform the signs with it."

Did you see how Moses so politely put the focus on what he felt he could not do. He was "disability focused" and not "ability focused". I understand how he felt. I disqualified myself from authoring a book because I am dyslexic. How could I author a book? I cannot spell. I can hear God list the many ways I could have overcome this challenge. I didn't when I heard God say, "Mike we have spell check now!" But, I know he must have said it. Therefore, we must do our reality checks. If I am to reach my 100%, what do I have to do to overcome my barriers? What is it that I am letting get in the way of this opportunity? Please note that God really became upset with Moses, because he focused on his disability and not his ability. Moreover, he questioned God's judgment of him being the one for this moment. Notice how God did not take kindly to Moses questing His judgement. His anger was more at Moses' lack of appreciation for his abilities. I know I have elicited this type of reaction from many of my "Because Of" people when I would put myself down.

    Not only will your "Because Of" people help you to work through this process, but your "In Spite Of" people can play a role in opening your eyes to your scotomas. I have been more motivated at times by those who have said "I could not" than I was by those who said, "I could". That is why we must be conscious of the process of finding our 100%. It allows us to process what is being presented to us and how we should respond. Moses was presented with an opportunity by, no less than, God himself. Moses still questioned God's easement of his abilities. He tried to convince God that he had made a mistake.

    Now, we probably have not had this type of encounter with God. However, we have had this with a teacher, coach, supervisor, professor, or mentor. Our reaction to a promotion was like that of Moses'. "You have picked the wrong person". God gave Moses a staff as a physical reminder that he was not alone in his journey. That is why we need to gather our "Because Of" people to remind us we are not alone on this journey. It must be noted that we sometimes react as negatively to "Because Of" people as we do "In Spite Of" people.

Why is this so? It is because of our scotomas. Whenever we are introduced to new possibilities, we are conditioned to default our self-view to the perceived faults and shortcomings that we feel disqualifies us from the opportunity. We do not reflect on our successes at first. We are conditioned to have negative self-talk. That is why it is so important to engage in self-affirmations. Our affirmations must be based on realistic and honest evaluation of our abilities. We must eliminate the truly unrealistic goals from the realistic. We hide behind unrealistic goals to prevent us from facing our fear of seeking what is possible. I am amazed at how much time and energy I have put into pursuing things that would never lead me to my 100%. We can get very compatible with settling for less than our 100%. We are even willing to put more time into someone's else's journey. We can easily see their path to 100% while we are blinded to our own.

I do not believe that Moses fully bought into his abilities. Moses never made it to the Promised Land. In other words, he never made it to his 100%. Moses did not manage the unforeseen obstacles and barriers too well. Moses thought that the Israelites would stop complaining at some point and develop an "attitude of gratitude".

Conclusion

Well, we know how this turned out. After being given a vote of confidence by God, Moses was not prepared to see that the Israelites suffered from the same problem he had. They, too, had a lack of faith in their quest for 100%. The Promised Land was the destination, but the journey would take them through the wilderness. They, like Moses, wanted to reach the Promised Land without a challenge. I hope I have made this principle of life clear. It is not a question of if we will have unforeseen barriers and obstacles, but *when* will we have them. More importantly, are we prepared to respond?

I have not intentionally focused on speaking on what God can or will do, whether we have faith or not. I have placed the issue squarely with humanity. If you claim a Christian faith, you know to turn to God in a time of struggle. If you do not have a faith system, you know you have to assess the situation and produce a plan. However, if you have scotomas that blind you to all the interventions for your situation, you will miss options. Both groups are hindered in maximizing their responsibilities. I do not want to minimize the challenges we face. The Israelites faced thirst, hunger, and military attacks. Many of you are facing racism, sexual assault, death of a loved one, and persecution for sexual orientation The struggle is real. However, if we have no process in place to respond with, we will miss our Promised Land of 100%. The only guarantee in life is if you do not work for your 100%, you will not get it.

Remember I am writing about your 100%. A 100lbs of cotton and a 100lbs of steel both weigh 100lbs.

However, both 100lbs look different. You must keep the focus on what you have control over. We cannot be responsible for how others respond to our journey to our 100%. Lack of focus will derail and delay your process. You cannot be like Moses. Do not be angry at people who have not yet reached your level of enlightenment. We must keep the focus on our growth. Then, seek to share it with others. We must become role models of the process. The more we are conscious of how the process works, the better we can share it.

The beauty of "finding your 100%" is that you can share the message behind the concept of "Because Of" and "In Spite Of." I believe racism and discrimination against people with disabilities will diminish when we become conscious of these concepts. America and the world are in a serious battle over which one: "Because Of" or "In Spite Of" solutions. There is no disagreement on the fault lines. We are a divided society. The solutions are varied. People on both sides are angry. After the January 6 insurrection, we now know how fragile our democracy is. When I started this book, the 2020 presidential election had not been settled. Joe Biden would win the presidential election. However, Trump and his supporters would not and have not accepted his legitimate victory. Trump's insistence that he won is referred to as the "Big Lie".

The posing of the "Big Lie" is proving to be as much of a threat to democracy as Covid 19 was to our health. Except for a few Republicans you can count on one hand, the "Big Lie" has become a rallying call to his followers to justify denying the victories of anyone but

Conclusion

Trump and his people. These Neo-Fascists are in bed with White Supremacists and Qanon. I never thought I would witness the capitol being assaulted by Americans. This symbol and the aspirations of hope, who so many have fought for and died for, were desiccated. The whole world saw, and our enemies cheered as we watched it in real time on the television. Police were killed and injured. So many put their lives on the line to be the only barrier between anarchy and democracy. The spirit of divisiveness and hatred was on full display.

    At the time I started this book, George Floyd had just been murdered by Derek Chauvin. He had not yet been charged and tried in a court of law. Floyd's murder was well documented on video. Had it not been for the bravery of Darnell Frazier, the conviction and sentencing of Chauvin may have never come. George Floyd's struggles in life would have disqualified him for justice. White America, thanks to Darrnell, saw what we have known to be true, Black Men are seen as a threat to be dealt with by any means necessary. We are now seeking solutions, while many still cling to the notion that no problems exist.

    Many young Black youths are no longer interested in incremental change. They want to see big changes; they are loud and active. They have begun to question and even reject the teachings and methods of Dr. King. They reject Christianity based on how it has been and still is used to justify racism and discrimination. I understand their reaction to things that have not changed fast enough in America. I. too, am angry and disappointed at how slow change has come. I am tired of having a conversation

Conclusion

around how much more we have to do to "...form a more perfect union". However, because I follow Jesus and not a church, which is what I consider to be proper theology, my response is still that what was taught by Dr. King. "If we seek an eye for an eye and teeth for teeth, we will have a world full of blind and toothless people."

I do not think that Dr. King's non-violent message takes away or dilutes the sense of urgency that youth have for change. Please read Dr. King's Letter from Birmingham Jail. The youth of today have no idea how oppressive and dangerous it was in America in the 50's and 60's. Believe me, it is much less dangerous today than it was in Dr. King's lifetime. The sacrifice and consequences were much more severe than they are now. This does not make light of the challenges we still face. However, there was no social media, video phones, or cable news. There were no laws on the books that even allowed for justice.

We embraced a pure view of Christianity that was not espoused by the white Evangelical Christian Church. We never saw slavery or Jim Crow as the will of God. This was challenged in our churches and schools. You would have had to live under this repressive system to fully appreciate the success of the Civil Rights Movement. Our brand of Christianity will not allow us to use hate to motivate. We understand that racism is a part of a bigger problem. We understand that humanity has a fallen nature, in need of redemption. That is why the Civil Rights Movement also addressed economic self-sufficiency. The Civil Rights movement saw education as the route to escaping poverty. If I didn't know better, to hear someone talk of the relationship between the Black Church and the perversion of Christianity, you would think we were in total agreement. I will admit the Black Church has had overlapping doctorial views on how we should treat the LGBTQ community. This is a place where the Black Church has begun to reexamine its stance as it relates to civil rights. However, the Black Church has been in the forefront of standing up for civil rights in the Black and Brown communities.

It is very easy to see our ancestors as weak for not having more of a violent response to racism. This generation of activists have so many more rights and tools to be more aggressive. However, our ancestors knew that violence is not the answer for long term change. This is not to say that it is not a time and place for self-defense. But, if we are trying to change evil, we cannot use it.

One of my criticisms of the Black Lives Matter (BLM) movement is its failure to address Black on Black crime. We cannot just address police reform without addressing how self-hate is killing more Black and Brown people than the police. We can do both at the same time, and we can do it without blaming and shaming Black and Brown people.

I cannot remember where or when I was introduced to the concept of internalized racism. I know it was at a conference I attended in Savannah, Georgia, on addressing the needs of students who were in alternative schools. However, I would like to share this definition of internalized racism by Donna Bivens:

Conclusion

Donna Bivens provides this definition of internalized racism in her chapter from Flipping the Script: White Privilege and Community Building on "What Is Internalized Racism?": "As people of color are victimized by racism, we internalize it. That is, we develop ideas, beliefs, actions and behaviors that support or collude with racism. This internalized racism has its own systemic reality and its own negative consequences in the lives and communities of people of color. More than just a consequence of racism, then, internalized racism is a systemic oppression in reaction to racism that has a life of its own. In other words, just as there is a system in place that reinforces the power and expands the privilege of white people, there is a system in place that actively discourages and undermines the power of people and communities of color and mires us in our own oppression..."

"...Because race is a social and political construct that comes out of particular histories of domination and exploitation between Peoples, people of colors' internalized racism often lead to great conflict among and between them as other concepts of power-such as ethnicity, culture, nationality and class-are collapsed in misunderstanding. ... Putting forward this definition of internalized racism that is systemic and structural is not intended to 'blame the victim.' It is meant to point out the unique work that people of color must do within ourselves and our communities to really address racism and white privilege. As experiences of race and structural racism become more confusing, complex, and obscured,

it is imperative that people of color explore and deepen our understanding of internalized racism. As more anti-racist white people become clearer about whiteness, white privilege... people of color are freed up to look beyond our physical and psychological trauma from racism."

Fundamentals, Core Concepts, Internalized Racism (racialequitytools.org)

When we accept racism subconsciously, we have developed a scotoma. It allows us to justify gang activity and dealing drugs in our communities. We have bought into capitalism by any means necessary. We began to claim colors and territories. We can demean our women and abandon our children without taking responsibility. This type of scotoma must be addressed as strongly as police reform. Therefore, I am against abolishing the police. We need intervention and prevention of crime.

I have spent my entire life working on the prevention side of the equation. I have attacked this issue without fear of failure. I am aware of the possibility and purpose of failure. I put to memory one of Teddy Roosevelt's quotes on this subject when I decided to be a "Because Of" person in the matter:

"It is not the critic who counts; not the man who points out how the strong man stumbles, or where the doer of deeds could have done them better. The credit belongs to the man who is actually in the arena, whose face is marred by dust and sweat and blood; who strives valiantly;

Conclusion

who errs, who comes short again and again, because there is no effort without error and shortcoming; but who does actually strive to do the deeds; who knows great enthusiasms, the great devotions; who spends himself in a worthy cause; who at the best knows in the end the triumph of high achievement, and who at the worst, if he fails, at least fails while daring greatly, so that his place shall never be with those cold and timid souls who neither know victory nor defeat."
— **Theodore Roosevelt**

The purpose of this book is twofold:

1. To help the reader seek their 100%
2. To help the reader become an intentional "Because Of" person who helps others on their journey to their 100%

We must see and be prepared to address the entire battlefield. It cannot be an either/or approach. It must be holistic, regardless of the ugliness in facing reality. I remember asking my students one day at the charter school I started, to look around and tell me if they saw any KKK members or anyone standing in the way of them getting an education. If not, then any success or failure was on them. I then stated that this school was set-up to address and destroy any barriers to their success. I am sure my former students will attest to my fierceness in protecting and supporting them.

I addressed violence in my community. I rewarded them by hosting concerts if we had no instances of violence in the school. Thanks to my adopted nephew, Kelevin Hamler (A.K.A. Tooly), I was able to get the Ying Yang Twins and DJ Smurf to perform in the gym at Central High School in Talbotton Georgia. This concert drew students from all surrounding areas. Prior to the concert, I met with gang leaders to get a commitment that this would not be a night of violence. After the concert, Tooly and I drove around the community to thank the gang leaders for respecting what I was trying to do in the community. There was not one instance of violence that night. The youth got to see and meet one of the hottest Rap acts in the world, right in little old Talbotton. The point is that our solutions must be boots on the ground and based on the realization of what power we have to make things better.

    Ask yourself this one question: what would the world look like without racism? Walk around that world and listen to the conversations. Walk around that world and look at how problems are solved. Look at how communities are set up. Visit the schools and see what is being taught. Listen to the sermons coming out of churches and see if the actions of the church match the sermons. Once you have finished your hypothetical exploration, please tell me if it did not look like a potential "Because Of" world. That is the point of this book. We must do it one step at a time. No law can change the heart. We must create examples of change, and hopefully others will follow suit. I am not trying to say this is a magic process. It is not. It places the responsibility squarely on everyone. If followed properly, we will be able to tell the "Because Of" people apart from the "In Spite Of" people. I am fully

Conclusion

aware that I cannot change the world by myself. However, I can change the part of the world I operate in. I can make a difference where I can make a difference. That is my goal. That is my dream.

My brother, Darryl, taught a class this summer on one of Jesus's miracles at his church's vacation bible school. He shared his lesson with me and said I should include it in the book. We both agreed it was one of the greatest miracles that Jesus performed. The miracle we refer to is when he feeds more than five thousand people with only five loaves of bread and two fish.

John 6:5-13

5 Jesus soon saw a huge crowd of people coming to look for him. Turning to Philip, he asked, "Where can we buy bread to feed all these people?" 6 He was testing Philip, for he already knew what he was going to do.
7 Philip replied, "Even if we worked for months, we wouldn't have enough money to feed them!"
8 Then Andrew, Simon Peter's brother, spoke up. 9 "There's a young boy here with five barley loaves and two fish. But what good is that with this huge crowd?"
10 "Tell everyone to sit down," Jesus said. So, they all sat down on the grassy slopes. (The men alone numbered about 5,000.) 11 Then Jesus took the loaves, gave thanks to God, and distributed them to the people. Afterward he did the same with the fish. And they all ate as much as they wanted. 12 After everyone was full, Jesus told his disciples, "Now gather the leftovers, so that nothing is wasted."

13 So they picked up the pieces and filled twelve baskets with scraps left by the people who had eaten from the five barley loaves.
NLT

    Jesus used the boy's lunch of two fish and five loaves and met the needs of over five thousand people. I would like to focus on the little boy's willingness to share 100% of his lunch. He must have had a childlike faith to believe his 100% contribution could meet the needs of so many. I wonder how many people moved away from him and his smelly fish. I wonder what Jesus must have said that touched him enough to see this view of himself. Had Jesus opened his vision of what his 100% was. I will admit that this is speculation on my part. Nevertheless, we do have a record that he gave up his lunch and more than 5000 were fed. And there were leftovers to boot! As my brother pointed out to me, "God always gives us more than we can believe." We must understand how our 100% can be multiplied. Give this life all that you have, and you will find your 100% will go a lot farther than you could imagine.

    People must understand: it is not about pouring into a person, but pulling what is needed out of a person.

Michael C Biggs, Sr

ABOUT THE AUTHOR

Mike Biggs is a man who had to learn to take care of himself just as well as he did of others. He's served God in the pulpit, family, military, classroom, and in business. He now shares those experiences with the world in writing now. Mike has learned from the best in his field of ministry/life coaching. The principle of sharing knowledge and skills with others has never been an issue. However, his time in the military stripped him of understanding how to personally navigate civilian life. It would take years for him to get back his "Civilian Mind."

Mike would learn that finding your 100 percent is not a destination but a process that has to be repeated throughout life. It is a process, once mastered, that must be shared and not hoardered. Mike faced his challenges and now shares a process that can be duplicated in the lives of his readers. He does not imply that life is not difficult ,but declares that each of us are uniquely equipped to respond to the challenges that life brings.